Prof. Marcão

Marcus Vinícius Pinto

Become an Internet Millionaire!

Learn about and put into practice the best ways to make money online.

© **Copyright 2024 - All rights reserved.**

The information provided herein is stated to be true and consistent, wherein any liability, in terms of inattention or otherwise, for any use or abuse of any policies, processes or guidance contained herein is the sole and absolute responsibility of the reader.

Under no circumstances shall any legal liability or fault be maintained against the authors for any repair, damage or monetary loss due to the information contained herein, whether directly or indirectly.

The authors own all copyrights to this work.

Legal Issues

This book is copyrighted. This is for personal use only. You may not alter, distribute, or sell any part or the contents of this book without the consent of the authors or copyright owner. If this is violated, legal action may be initiated.

The information contained herein is offered for informational purposes only and is therefore universal. The presentation of the information is without contract or any kind of warranty.

The trademarks that are used in this book are used for examples or composition of arguments. This use is done without any consent, and the publication of the trademark is without permission or endorsement from the trademark owner and are the property of the owners themselves, not affiliated herewith.

The images that are present here without authorship citation are public domain images or were created by the authors of the book.

Disclaimer:

Please note that the information contained in this document is for educational and entertainment purposes only. Every effort has been made to provide complete, accurate, up-to-date and reliable information. No warranty of any kind is express or implied.

By reading this text, the reader agrees that under no circumstances are the authors liable for any losses, direct or indirect, incurred as a result of the use of the information contained in this book, including, but not limited to, errors, omissions, or inaccuracies.

ISBN: 9798320939872
Selo editorial: Independently published

Foreword

Welcome to the world of digital entrepreneurship, where the opportunities are vast and the potential for growth is limitless. "Be an Internet Millionaire" is not just another book about making money online, it is a comprehensive and dynamic guide that will lead you down a path of discovery and fulfillment in the virtual universe.

Exploring everything from the foundations of digital marketing to advanced monetization strategies, this book is a compendium of essential knowledge for those who want to thrive in the information age. As you dive into the following pages, you'll be introduced to a variety of ways to monetize your time and talent on the internet, whether it's creating digital products, providing specialized services, or tapping into promising niche markets.

Figure 1 - Be a millionaire of the virtual world.

Each chapter in this book provides valuable insights, practical examples, and clear guidance to help you navigate an ocean of online opportunities. From developing skills in areas such as SEO, affiliate marketing, content production, and social media management to creating a strong personal brand and building an engaged audience, you'll find in this book the support you need to take the first steps towards digital success.

With the technological revolution in full swing, there's no better time to launch yourself into the world of online entrepreneurship and reap the rewards of innovation and creativity. Not only does this book offer a roadmap to success on the internet, but it also serves as a mentor that will guide you on your journey of professional growth and fulfillment.

Get ready for a transformative experience filled with learning, challenges, and achievements. "Be an Internet Millionaire" is more than a book, it's an invitation to take control of your financial destiny and explore the full potential that the digital age has to offer. The revolution has only just begun – and you have the power to be part of that transformation.

I'm sure the content here can make a big difference in your life.

Happy reading!
Happy learning!
Earn big money!

Prof. Marcão - Marcus Vinícius Pinto

Digital Influencer
Entrepreneurship Specialist, Soft Skills,
product pricing and neuromarketing.
Founder, CEO, teacher and pedagogical advisor of
MVP Consult.

*To my beloved Andrea,
that may not always be right,
But he's always right.*
Prof. Marcão – Marcus Pinto

Summary

1	**YOUR NEW WORKPLACE.**	**19**
1.1	HOW ABOUT BEING AN INTERNET PROFESSIONAL.	20
1.2	HOW TO USE THIS BOOK.	22
2	**QUESTION: DO YOU KNOW WHAT IT'S LIKE TO BE AN INTERNET PROFESSIONAL?**	**25**
2.1	BUT WHAT DOES IT MEAN TO BE AN INTERNET PROFESSIONAL?	25
3	**WAY 1 – MAKE MONEY AS A DIGITAL PRODUCER.**	**29**
3.1	TOP INFOPRODUCTS TO PRODUCE OR SELL	31
3.1.1	E-BOOKS.	31
3.1.2	DIGITAL COURSES.	34
3.1.3	PODCASTS OU VIDEOCASTS.	37
3.1.4	AUDIOBOOKS.	40
3.1.5	SUBSCRIPTION PROGRAMS.	43
3.1.6	ELECTRONIC MAGAZINES.	44
3.1.7	WHITE PAPER.	44
3.1.8	WEBINARS.	45
3.1.9	CREATION OF INFOGRAPHICS AND TEMPLATES.	47
3.2	HOW TO BECOME A DIGITAL PRODUCER?	48
3.3	WHAT ARE THE BEST NICHES TODAY?	50
3.4	BE AN AUTHORITY AND SELL MORE	51
3.5	ADVANTAGES AND DISADVANTAGES OF BEING A DIGITAL PRODUCER	51
3.6	ARE THERE CHALLENGES TO OVERCOME?	52
3.7	HOW MUCH DOES A DIGITAL PRODUCER MAKE?	52
4	**WAY 2 – MAKE MONEY AS A BLOGGER.**	**54**
4.1	IDEAS TO MAKE MONEY BLOGGING.	55
4.2	SALE OF ADVERTISING.	56
4.3	MAKE POSTINGS ON YOUR BLOG.	56
4.4	ADD YOUR OPINION	57
4.5	ONLINE COURSES AND E-BOOKS.	57
4.6	WHAT ABOUT SELLING DIGITAL PRODUCTS?	59

4.7	**STRATEGIES TO MAKE YOUR ENDEAVOR EASIER.**	**60**
4.7.1	CHOOSE YOUR NICHE ACCORDING TO YOUR GOALS AND YOUR KNOWLEDGE.	60
4.7.2	BE A CROSS-PLATFORM BLOGGER	61
4.7.3	BE A SLAVE TO YOUR EDITORIAL CALENDAR.	62
4.7.4	HAVE A CONSOLIDATED NETWORK.	63
4.7.5	PARTNER WITH OTHER BLOGGERS.	64
4.7.6	BUILD ENGAGEMENT ON SOCIAL MEDIA.	64
4.7.7	LEARN SEO TECHNIQUES – IT MAKES ALL THE DIFFERENCE.	65
4.7.8	INVEST IN PAID TRAFFIC.	65
4.7.9	KNOW HOW TO ANALYZE PERFORMANCE INDEXES.	66
4.7.10	BE AN ETERNAL PERFECTIONIST.	66
4.8	**ADVANTAGES AND DISADVANTAGES OF BEING A BLOGGER**	**67**
5	**WAY 3 – EARN MONEY AS A VIRTUAL ASSISTANT.**	**69**
6	**WAY 4 - MAKE MONEY AS A VIDEO EDITOR**	**72**
6.1	**IS IT BETTER TO BE A VIDEO EDITOR WITH A STEADY JOB OR A FREELANCER?**	**73**
6.2	**WHERE TO WORK?**	**73**
6.3	**TRAINING AND SALARY.**	**74**
7	**WAY 5 – EARN MONEY WITH AFFILIATE PROGRAM.**	**75**
7.1	**HOW DOES IT WORK?**	**76**
7.1.1	INVESTOR AFFILIATE.	78
7.1.2	AUTHORITY AFFILIATE.	79
7.2	**POSITIVES AND NEGATIVES OF AFFILIATE PROGRAMS**	**81**
7.2.1	POSITIVES – GO IN FAITH!	81
7.2.2	NEGATIVES – OPEN YOUR EYES!	83
7.3	**WHAT NOW? WHICH PROGRAM TO CHOOSE?**	**83**
8	**WAY 6 – MAKE MONEY AS AN ONLINE FREELANCER.**	**85**
8.1	**HOW TO SUCCEED AS A FREELANCER?**	**86**
8.2	**IS IT NECESSARY TO HAVE A COLLEGE DEGREE TO WORK AS A FREELANCER?**	**87**
8.3	**ADVANTAGES AND DISADVANTAGES.**	**87**
8.4	**HOW TO GET A FREELANCE JOB.**	**88**
8.4.1	JOBS OF A FREELANCER.	89
8.5	**WHAT IS THE IDEAL PLATFORM?**	**90**

8.6	DON'T WAIT FOR YOUR CHANCES TO FALL FROM THE SKY.	91
9	**WAY 7 – MAKE MONEY WITH AUDIO BOOK NARRATION.**	**92**
9.1	TAKE THIS CASE.	92
9.2	PAULO BETTI.	93
9.3	COURSE.	94
9.4	CHRISTIAN NICHE.	94
9.5	PLATFORMS.	95
9.6	HOW MUCH DOES A BOOK NARRATOR MAKE?	96
9.7	HOW CAN YOU GET STARTED?	96
9.8	HOW TO CHOOSE THE IDEAL STUDIO FOR PRODUCTION?	97
10	**WAY 8 - MAKE MONEY WITH AN ONLINE STORE.**	**97**
10.1	HOW TO WORK WITH ONLINE STORES.	98
10.2	WHAT DOES THE CUSTOMER EXPECT FROM THE ONLINE STORE'S CUSTOMER SERVICE?	98
10.3	TYPES OF ONLINE STORES.	99
10.4	DIFFERENTIAL.	99
10.5	ADVANTAGES AND DISADVANTAGES.	102
10.6	CHOICE OF PRODUCT MIX.	104
10.7	STEPS TO CREATE YOUR ONLINE STORE.	104
10.7.1	DEFINITION OF THE NAME OF THE ONLINE STORE.	104
10.7.2	COMPETITOR ANALYSIS.	104
10.7.3	SELECTION OF THE E-COMMERCE PLATFORM	105
10.7.4	CUSTOMIZATION OF THE ONLINE STORE	105
10.7.5	INCLUSION OF PRODUCT IMAGES AND DESCRIPTIONS	105
10.7.6	SECURITY FOR THE ONLINE STORE	106
10.8	ONCE THE STORE IS SET UP, IT'S TIME TO ADVERTISE THE BUSINESS.	108
10.8.1	THE BIG COST OF AN ONLINE STORE IS IN THE PROMOTION OF THE BUSINESS.	108
10.8.2	THE COST OF PROMOTING THE ONLINE STORE.	109
10.8.3	CUSTOMER JOURNEY MAPPING.	109
10.8.4	AD SPEND.	109
10.8.5	INVESTMENT IN MOBILE.	110
10.9	CLARITY IN THE PRIVACY POLICY.	110
11	**WAY 9 – MAKE MONEY ON BUYING AND SELLING SITES.**	**111**
11.1	TO BE A GOOD INTERNET MARKETER, PAY ATTENTION TO THESE TIPS.	113
11.1.1	DECIDE WHAT YOU WANT TO BUY AND SELL.	113

11.1.2	RESEARCH THE MARKET.	114
11.1.3	FIND A SUPPLIER TO SOURCE YOUR GOODS.	114
11.1.4	BUY CHEAP, SELL FOR A BETTER PRICE.	114
11.2	BUYING AND SELLING SITES ON THE INTERNET.	115
12	**FORM 10 - CONTENT CREATOR FOR THE WEB.**	**118**
12.1	UNDERSTAND THE ORIGIN OF THE PROFESSION.	119
12.2	THE CURRENT SCENARIO - CO-CREATION.	119
12.3	WHAT ARE THE ADVANTAGES OF HIRING A CONTENT CREATOR?	125
12.4	REACH.	125
12.5	NEW CONSUMPTION RULES.	126
12.6	IT'S NOT ALL SPOTLIGHTS: THERE ARE LAWS!	126
12.7	AND HOW TO GET STARTED?	127
13	**WAY 11 – MAKE MONEY AS SOCIAL MEDIA.**	**128**
13.1	WHAT THIS PROFESSIONAL IS AND WHAT HE DOES.	129
13.2	WHAT DOES SOCIAL MEDIA MEAN?	130
13.3	WHAT DOES A SOCIAL MEDIA PROFESSIONAL DO?	130
13.4	WHAT IS THE ACADEMIC BACKGROUND OF THIS PROFESSIONAL?	131
13.5	THE ROUTINE OF A SOCIAL MEDIA.	131
13.6	TOOLS AND SOFTWARE USED BY SOCIAL MEDIA.	133
13.7	HOW MUCH DOES A SOCIAL MEDIA PROFESSIONAL MAKE?	133
13.8	WHAT IS THE JOB MARKET LIKE?	134
13.9	TOP WAYS TO MAKE MONEY AS A SOCIAL MEDIA.	134
13.10	BUT THINK ABOUT IT!	135
14	**WAY 12 – MAKE MONEY AS AN SEO MANAGER.**	**137**
14.1	HOW TO BECOME AN SEO MANAGER?	138
14.2	DUTIES OF THE SEO ANALYST.	139
14.3	LEARNING PATH TO BECOMING AN SEO ANALYST	140
14.4	REASONS FOR A COMPANY TO HIRE AN SEO.	141
14.5	**ADVANTAGES** AND DISADVANTAGES OF BEING AN SEO MANAGER.	141
15	**FORM 13 - PAID TRAFFIC MANAGER.**	**143**
15.1	WHY HAVE A TRAFFIC MANAGER IN THE COMPANY?	147

15.2	CLASSIFICATION OF TRAFFIC MANAGERS?	148
15.3	HOW MUCH DOES A PAID TRAFFIC MANAGER MAKE?	149

16   FORMA 14 - COPYWRITER.   151

16.1	WHAT SKILLS ARE NEEDED?	151
16.2	HOW CAN ONE ENTER THIS FIELD?	152
16.3	WHAT DO COPYWRITERS WRITE?	154
16.4	HOW MUCH DOES A COPYWRITER MAKE?	155

17   FORM 15 - IMAGE EDITING.   156

17.1	WHAT SKILLS DOES A PHOTO EDITOR NEED?	157
17.2	WHAT ABOUT DIGITAL SKILLS?	158
17.3	WHO IS THE SUPERVISOR OF A PHOTO EDITOR?	158
17.4	WHAT DOES IT TAKE TO EXCEL IN THIS POSITION?	158
17.5	A PRECIOUS TIP.	158
17.6	HOW CAN I ENTER THIS FIELD?	158
17.7	ADVANTAGES OF PHOTO EDITING FOR BUSINESSES.	159
17.8	SALARY RANGE & SALARY FLOOR 2022	161

18   FORM 16 - SALE OF PHOTOGRAPHS.   163

18.1	HOW TO SELL PHOTOS ONLINE THROUGH IMAGE LIBRARIES.	163
18.2	BEST SITES TO SELL YOUR PHOTOS ONLINE.	164
18.3	TIPS TO MAKE EXTRA MONEY SELLING PHOTOS.	166
18.4	HOW TO SELL YOUR PHOTOS AS PRINTS	166
18.5	USE A PHOTO HOSTING SITE	167
18.6	SELL PHOTOS ON SOCIAL MEDIA	167

19   FORM 17 - ONLINE PRIVATE TUTOR.   168

19.1	WHAT ARE THE QUALIFICATIONS FOR AN ONLINE PRIVATE TUTORING JOB?	169
19.2	WHAT TECHNOLOGY IS NEEDED TO WORK AS AN ONLINE TUTOR?	169
19.3	WHAT IS THE PROFILE OF THE ONLINE PRIVATE TUTOR?	170
19.4	HOW MUCH DOES A PRIVATE TUTOR MAKE.	170

20   FORMA 18 – DROPSHIPPING.   171

20.1	How to Start Dropshipping in 7 Steps	172
20.2	How to Create a Dropshipping Website	173
20.3	Benefits of dropshipping	173
20.4	Disadvantages of dropshipping.	175

21 FORM 19 – PRINT ON DEMAND. 177

21.1	How do I start my own print-on-demand business?	179
21.2	Is print on demand profitable?	179
21.3	How Do You Price Print on Demand Products?	179

22 MEET THE AUTHOR. 180

22.1	Prof. Marcão - Marcus Vinícius Pinto.	180
22.2	Some books published by Prof. Marcão.	182
22.3	Books on Open Data by Prof. Marcão.	184
22.4	How to contact Prof. Marcão.	185

Index of Figures

Figure 1 - Be a millionaire of the virtual world. 5
Figure 2 – ARPANET computers. 19
Figure 3 – The Internet is really amazing! 21
Figure 4 – How to use this book. 23
Figure 5 Where am I, where am I going? 24
Figure 6 – The 4 dominant characteristics of the Internet professional. 26
Figure 7 – The camera is the faithful companion of many internet professions. 27
Figure 8 - The digital producer and their cameras. 29
Figure 9 – Fundamental steps to become a digital producer. 30
Figure 10 – E-books are the new way to bring knowledge to readers. 31
Figure 11 – E-learning is a new way to learn from home. 36
Figure 12 – Podcasts are gaining more and more space. 38
Figure 13 - Audiobook – listen to a book. 40
Figure 14 – AAC has revolutionized access to digital content. 42
Figure 15 – How about a Webinar with Elon Musk? 46
Figure 16 – Examples of digital products. 48
Figure 17 – An online student. A sign of the times. 49
Figure 18 – Make a lot of money. The dream possible. 53
Figure 19 – A Youtuber at work. 54
Figure 20 – How to structure a blog. 55
Figure 21 – A student in an online course. 58
Figure 22 – The niche funnel. 61
Figure 23 – Example of a legendary editorial. 62
Figure 24 – Conversion cycle. 63
Figure 25 – Good initiatives to have a list of your visitors. 64
Figure 26 - Blogging for a living can be difficult. 67
Figure 27 – Virtual assistant is the profession of the moment. 69
Figure 28 – Well-done video editing is a big challenge. 72
Figure 29 – The mouse is the buying tool. 75
Figure 30 – Criteria for participation in an affiliate program. 76
Figure 31 – Percentage of commissions. 77
Figure 32 – It is very important to evaluate positive and negative points. 81
Figure 33- The trophy is your income. 82
Figure 34 – The happiness of the Freelancer: delivering the work. 85
Figure 35 - The freelancer's question: which platform to choose? 91
Figure 36 – Customer service makes all the difference. 101
Figure 37 – Add to cart. 107
Figure 38 – Success tips for those who buy and those who sell. 112
Figure 39- The creator cloud. 118
Figure 40 - Co-creation allows for collaborative work. 120
Figure 41 – Digital influencer. 124
Figure 42 – The universe of Social Media work. 128
Figure 43 – Social media. 130
Figure 44 – The world of social media work. 135

Figure 45 - Be an SEO manager. _____ *137*
Figure 46 – The traffic manager has a lot of responsibility. _____ *143*
Figure 47 "And the salary, oh! _____ *150*
Figure 48 – Essential skills of a Copywriter. _____ *152*
Figure 49 – Image editing requires professional software. _____ *156*
Figure 50 – The photo editor is not a photographer, but it works miracles. _____ *157*
Figure 51 - The dropshipping cycle. _____ *171*
Figure 52 - The print-on-demand cycle. _____ *178*
Figure 53- The Value of Human Capital. _____ *180*
Figure 54 – Some books by Prof. Marcão. _____ *182*
Figure 55 – Some more books by Prof. Marcão. _____ *183*
Figure 56 – Books on Open Data. _____ *184*
Figure 57 – Let's value teachers. _____ *186*

"It's the steps that make the paths."

MARIO QUINTANA

1 YOUR NEW WORKPLACE.

The early days of most technological revolutions are dominated by builders, and there is typically a lack of deep conceptualization and lucid explanation. The creation of ARPAnet, the first incarnation of the Internet, is no exception to this rule.

> ARPAnet (Advanced Research Projects Agency Network, Portuguese) was the first computer network, built in 1969 as a robust means to transmit classified military data and to interconnect research departments throughout the United States.

Many years passed before great thinkers delved deeper and reflected on the implications of the digital revolution in the lives of all of us.

Figure 2 – ARPANET computers.

Every day more and more people turn to the Internet for information and a contingent, growing every day, is discovering in the large network an alternative to make money. That's right!

These are people who, for one reason or another, are looking for new ways to achieve financial independence, freedom and flexible hours. They are looking for a job opportunity to replace a lost position. Or simply a way to have a supplementary income.

If you came to this book with some of these goals, or even if your goals are different, know that you will find here the 19 best ways to make money in the Internet universe.

And don't worry! I don't think it's necessary for you to have a great deal of knowledge about technology, marketing, or business administration. There are no constraints other than your willingness to start a career and work.

These forms of work were selected among several because they are accessible to most people. You will learn how to make money from your own home, with your cell phone or your home computer, with practical and simple ideas.

Even if not all the ways will suit your profile, I have no doubt that some of them will be perfect for you. That's not even taking into account that all these ideas of making money on the internet are challenging, legal, and honest. No pyramids, no lying promises, or anything like that.

The only essential requirement is that you are willing to work with focus and dedication to achieve the results YOU want.

1.1   How about being an internet professional.

The Internet is currently a powerful platform that goes beyond helping us find news, texts, and connect with distant friends and loved ones.

More than ever, it is a platform that allows us to undertake and consolidate new careers. The only condition is that it is done in the right way.

There are many ways to make money online, such as affiliate marketing, creating online stores, blogging, etc. A good reason to jump into this endeavor is that this could be your chance to get out of the race for a job. Failing to submit to stressful and hopeless interviews.

Here's your chance to pursue your financial freedom and shake off torturous bonds with employers who exploit more than they remunerate.

Figure 3 – The Internet is really amazing!

The Internet is now a platform on which many people converge to sell their labor power. And if you're thinking about starting an online career, then you've got the right stuff in front of your eyes!

You'll agree with me that not everyone needs an office job to make a living. In fact, more and more professionals work from home and earn their living legally through content on the internet. Thousands of people are already living like this, whether it's through their blogs, YouTube channels, or becoming influencers.

In this book I will guide you on how you can be one of those people.

You can start your business from your home RIGHT NOW.

You can start making money from now on.

You will have the possibility to have a better life, with less stress and more freedom.

Even if not all of these ways fit your profile, I have no doubt that some of them will be perfect for you. Not to mention that all these ideas of making money on the internet are legal and honest, no pyramids, lying promises or things like that.

The 19 ways to make money online that we are going to deal with are:

1. Digital Production.
2. Blogger.
3. Virtual assistant.
4. Video editor.
5. Affiliate program.
6. Freelancer.
7. Audio Book Narration.
8. Shop.
9. Buying and selling sites.
10. Web Content Creator.
11. Social Media.
12. SEO management.
13. Paid Traffic Management.
14. Copywriter.
15. Image Editing.
16. Sale of Photographs.
17. Online private tutor.
18. Dropshipping.
19. Print-on-demand.

Remember, the only necessary requirement is to be willing to work with focus and dedication to achieve the results you want.

An interesting thing to note in the job market is that with the passage of time and the advancement of technology, it is natural for two situations to happen:

- ✓ Some professions, which have been around for a long time, are extinguished or replaced by machines.
- ✓ New professions and new job openings are emerging.

Here I will introduce you and explain how the new professions work so that you are ahead in the search for your financial gains.

Start!

1.2　How to use this book.

Here are proposals and analysis of the 19 ways to make money on the Internet that I consider most efficient, profitable and guaranteed.

Each shape is presented in a chapter. In it I present the following sections:

What it is to be a professional in the way dealt with in the section.
Checklist to validate that your personality is fit for purpose.
How the profession, represented by the form, works.
Differentials that you need to have or develop to be successful in form.
Existing niches to form on the Internet.
Advantages and disadvantages of being a fashion professional.
Challenges to be overcome.
How much does a fashion professional earn.

Figure 4 – How to use this book.

Of course, everything involves risks, learning, some financial investment and dedication, but by following my guidelines and observing the tips you have a great chance of being successful.

Thus, I suggest that you study the ways to select which ones seem most attractive to you and study a little more those that you have selected.

With this information, I believe you will have a lot of support to choose "the" way that will make a difference in your life. It is with it that you will make a lot of money and be successful.

And remember, there is no right or wrong choice. The future is in your hands.

Figure 5 Where am I, where am I going?

2   QUESTION: DO YOU KNOW WHAT IT'S LIKE TO BE AN INTERNET PROFESSIONAL?

It may seem strange to discuss this subject in a book, but it is better to clarify this point before we proceed to elucidate doubts or unfounded expectations.

I'm not here to sell you miracle formulas that will make you rich overnight practically without you moving a straw.

This is not the case!

I don't want to deceive you by saying that this is an easy path, but it sure is a possible path. It requires dedication and perseverance, but this challenge can bring you great rewards.

Yes, I'm stating that it won't be easy!

Most books and articles that deal with professions on the Internet promise that it will be the most peaceful thing in the world, but it is not.

I don't want to start our relationship with lies and snares. I want you to be fully aware that this path is possible with a lot of dedication and I will present you with everything you need to know to start your online adventure.

This book will be your guide and lead you in the right direction. Following the teachings presented here is the first step that will lead you to increase your revenue and create a successful business.

2.1   But what does it mean to be an Internet professional?

Being an Internet professional means working in an environment that doesn't physically exist. It doesn't have an office, a headquarters, a store. Your world is virtual. Your horizon of work is endless.

He is a professional who can produce and sell anything in the digital world, he can talk and write about whatever he wants.

It's being someone who has 4 dominant traits:

WILL TO WIN.

KNOWLEDGE.

PERSISTENCE

RESILIENCE.

Figure 6 – The 4 dominant characteristics of the Internet professional.

A phrase, attributed to Valdeci Nogueira, that translates very well what the will to win means for a professional in the digital world is:

> "The will to win makes anyone different from others because they are bold, intrepid and determined, which in practice is what makes all the difference between what is new and what is ordinary."

Knowledge is what will make the difference between being successful and being a loser. Considering that everything today is just a click away to be accessed, your knowledge needs to result in something that solves your customer's needs. Something that makes a difference in his life.

Persistence will ensure that you won't be overwhelmed by the numerous obstacles you'll need to overcome throughout your career. The world of the internet is unethical and with enormous competition. Your audience is loyal and seeks the lowest cost on everything.

Resilience is a strong partner of persistence, as it ensures that you will come out of the worst situations the same or better than before. It is the professional's ability to continue to thrive even in a hostile environment. But note that it is possible to consider resilience as something from the professional's context.

An author who deals with this topic is Boris Cyrulnik, . He proposes the concept that resilience is not an individual competence, but the result of the positive bonds that a person weaves with others within healthy living spaces. In other words, resilience embodies the strength of the professional's network.(Cyrulnik, 2004)

We can summarize then by stating that to be an Internet professional is to be someone who:

- works in an environment that doesn't exist;
- produces and sells anything;
- speak and write whatever he wants; and
- You need to have the will to win, knowledge, resilience and persistence.

Figure 7 – The camera is the faithful companion of many internet professions.

But let's take it easy. This does not mean that only a few people blessed by the gods can be these professionals. My goal here is to show you that you can make money on the Internet in various ways with almost no investment and without having to go to a very expensive college.

You'll choose the way you want to make money and I'll show you how to achieve your goals.

It's important to realize that regardless of which way you choose, you need to follow a code of behavior to avoid putting your endeavor at risk.

Already in 2010, the Internet professional was known as "professional 2.0" due to the fact that these people work "for" and "with" the Internet and proposed a code of behavior for these new professionals with 8 main items:

1. Respond to emails. Every email is important to your network, sales, and consulting.
2. Don't be late for meetings. Whether virtual or in-person, you need to be punctual.
3. Be articulate. You need to master the art of communication as this is an essential element in your arsenal.
4. Be stylish. Even if you work with a young audience, try to be a reference of elegance, even if your style is cooler.
5. Research and write. There is nothing more up-to-date and engaged than mastering the language, good manners and respect in communication.
6. Help those who ask for help with humility and sincerity. Always help those who come to you for some guidance and never play the superior. This is in very bad taste.
7. Meet deadlines every time. This makes sure that your authority is confirmed and you keep your customers and followers.
8. Cultivate the network. And always remember that network is not quantity. It's quality. Have in your circle people who really tell you something, who share subjects, interests, groups, ideas.

3 WAY 1 – MAKE MONEY AS A DIGITAL PRODUCER.

The Digital Producer is the person who is an expert or has advanced knowledge in a particular subject and has the desire to share what they know with the world through digital means.

The producer is 100% responsible for his success on the internet, having full control over his routine and productivity.

Figure 8 - The digital producer and their cameras.

As a consequence, by working correctly, using the right strategies, and having a digital product in demand in the market, the financial return can be great.

One point in favor of this type of work is the financial investment required to create a digital product. The investment for most products is extremely low.

Basically, you'll need:

- a computer with internet access;
- a cell phone;
- a tripod; and
- a microphone.

However, it will require you to have a lot of discipline and follow some fundamental steps.

1	Choose your niche market after a lot of analysis. Research trends and set goals.
2	Coldly analyze whether your knowledge can really be turned into a digital product.
3	See if there is demand for your product in the market. Research if there are already any products on the market similar to the one you want to create and how much it sells.
4	Choose the best format to deliver your digital product, such as e-book, video lessons, and audio.
5	Learn digital marketing strategies. Mastering these techniques makes all the difference.
6	Position yourself as an authority, produce content and make use of digital media to attract the audience that has the potential to be interested in your product.

Figure 9 – Fundamental steps to become a digital producer.

To help you with the initial analysis, I've brought you some examples.

- ✓ A teacher can increase the reach of their classes by creating online courses or taking live classes.
- ✓ A Digital Influencer can produce an e-book on how to become an influencer.
- ✓ An actor can grow their audience by recording audiobooks.
- ✓ A writer can diversify their work by producing a Youtube channel with book reviews.

Among the most common digital content to be produced by this type of professional are the following.

3.1 Top Infoproducts to Produce or Sell

3.1.1 E-books.

If you look up e-book in the dictionary, you'll find the following:

> *Noun. A book composed or converted to digital form for display on a computer screen or portable device.*

Pretty straightforward. An e-book; an e-book.

But here's the thing: if an e-book is a book in digital form that, technically speaking, qualifies a lot of things that aren't really e-books.

Figure 10 – E-books are the new way to bring knowledge to readers.

E-books are files that you can read on a digital device, a tablet, smartphone, computer, etc. But again, considering that e-books, like many other files, can be read on a device, in order for it to be considered an e-book, it needs to have some special characteristics.

A distinctive feature of an e-book is the fact that the text is not editable. An eBook should always be converted into a format that ensures it is not editable.

With thousands of people having access to it on digital devices, people could alter any content without the author's permission. Therefore, to qualify as a real ebook, the text must not be altered in any way, just like a paperback book.

Another important feature is that true e-books should be reflowable. This means that no matter what size screen you're viewing the ebook on, it will always fit on the screen. Text will remain formatted with line breaks, and chapters and images will be resized to fit the proportions of the device you're reading on.

There's one exception: PDFs[1]. Considering that PDFs can't be edited but aren't reflowable, they technically don't qualify as e-books because they don't meet this characteristic.

But with companies taking advantage of the ease of PDF downloads and distribution, PDFs have become "unofficial" e-books and are still widely used e-book formats.

If you search for ebook formats, you'll find several options. Dozens, in fact. However, the likelihood of actually using many of these formats is quite small.

To make it simple for you, let's take a look at the three that are known for their ease of use and ability to be used in a widely distributed format: EPUB, AZW, and PDF.

1. EPUB (.epub).

Epub is short for Electronic Publishing and was created by a consortium of companies called IDPF – International Digital Publishing Forum. Companies such as Adobe, Sony, Microsoft, among others, are part of the IDPF.

An EPUB, or electronic publication, is the most widely supported format and can be read on a variety of devices, including computers, smartphones, tablets, and most eReaders[2] (except Kindles[3]).

---

[1] PDF (Portable Document Format) is a file format developed by Adobe Systems to represent documents independently of the application, hardware, and operating system used to create them.
[2] An eReader (or electronic reader) is the name popularly given to readers of books, magazines, newspapers, and other documents in digital format.
[3] The Kindle is Amazon's e-reader. The appearance of the device may resemble a tablet, but the proposal is quite different. The Kindle is a digital book reader and, of course, it was designed especially for that.

EPUB files are reflowable, which makes them true e-books and easier to read on small devices.

2. AZW (.azw).

The AZW files were developed by Amazon for its Kindle eReaders. These files can store complex content such as bookmarks, annotations, and highlights.

But the use of AZW files is limited to Kindles or devices with Kindle apps. Also, they can only be accessed from Amazon's online bookstore.

3. PDF (.pdf).

A PDF, also known as a portable document format, isn't technically a true ebook according to our definition, but it's the format most people are familiar with.

Created by Adobe, PDFs are known for their ease of use and ability to maintain custom layouts. Because they retain their shape and are not reflowable, they can be difficult to read on a small screen. Despite this, they are still one of the most widely used eBook formats, especially by marketers.

3.1.2 Digital courses.

Digital courses are growing in popularity, especially with platforms like Udemy and Hotmart launching into mainstream acceptance.

But what are digital courses?

They are just like any other learning course you can find in a learning institute. Except they take place online and tend to be on much more specific subjects (e.g., how to invest in cryptocurrency for beginners) than those available at standard learning institutes.

Digital courses are also known as eLearning.

The accessibility of digital courses has solved a long-standing problem in adult education. You'll be hard-pressed to find someone who isn't interested in broadening their knowledge in a subject, and often the only thing that prevented a large number of prospective students from studying in the past was the inconvenience of attending classes and finding private tutors.

Today, thanks to the exploited potential of the internet and remote study, we can take courses on almost any subject from the comfort of our homes, after a day at work, or even on our morning commute.

Udemy is one of the market leaders in the increasingly popular field of online education, with a website of around 55,000 courses developed by 'instructors' enrolled on the site.

For a relatively small fee, users can take a course on Udemy that focuses on a variety of fields.

From learning how to 'master the Rubik's cube in four days', to 'building sacred relationships that stand the test of time', to 'how to make soap – making homemade soap for beginners'. With sites like Udemy, it seems like anyone can find their niche.

This brings us to the digital commerce behind eLearning. If you have a set of niche knowledge that you want to share on a subject, you can do so by setting up a digital course.

By using a reputable hosting site, you'll ensure that your authority is noticed, and you can start profiting from the education of others.

It's worth considering how you plan to engage your audience and your approach to becoming a calm yet informative educator. Once you've figured out the teaching style that will keep your students coming back, the sky's the limit!

Figure 11 – E-learning is a new way to learn from home.

Creating an eLearning course also helps your exposure and therefore the broadening of your other networks as well. Happy customers will be able to comfortably find you and your website, which will expand your traffic and reputation.

As with much of the information you share online, digital partnership comes into play. This means that all of your hard work is in the hands of your host site or your platform.

If you use Udemy to offer your digital course to a large audience, your course is subject to the whims of that site – they can remove it without notice or close its entire pages, costing you money and potential exposure.

Tip: Focus on finding your niche subject to share your knowledge with when creating a digital course.

It may seem intuitive to educate on a more general subject to increase your audience's catchment, but with such a dense field of competitors, it pays to be more intricate.

For example, if you're thinking of taking a course on 'Grow Your Social Media Presence', you might want to adjust it to 'Grow Your Social Media Presence on Twitter'.

3.1.3 Podcasts ou videocasts.

A podcast is the answer of the streaming era to radio. The dictionary definition of a podcast is a digital audio file that you can download or listen to over the internet. Its story explains why it's called a podcast, to begin with.

Podcasts are a form of media content that was developed in 2004 when former MTV host Adam Curry and software developer Dave Winer encoded the content to be processed by the iPodder.

The iPodder was a computer program that allowed the user to download internet radio broadcasts to their Apple iPod. That's when the term podcast was born and meaning, taking its name from a mix of 'iPod' and 'broadcasts'.

Today, podcasts are an extremely popular form of audio entertainment, and they have progressed beyond being downloadable radio shows.

Each podcast is a series created by a host and then published episode by episode online, where subscribers can then download and listen to each episode when it is released.

Unlike traditional methods of content production, such as TV and radio shows, podcasts are an affordable way for content creators to connect with an audience.

They're not regulated at the moment, which means you don't need a streaming license to publish podcast content.

Figure 12 – Podcasts are gaining more and more space.

Anyone with basic podcast equipment, such as a microphone, recording software, and a subscription to a hosting platform, can create their own show.

Monetizing a podcast is also becoming a reliable way to make a side or a full-time income, thanks to brand sponsorships, affiliate marketing, subscriptions, and paid content.

Are podcasts audio or video?

Podcasts started out as a full-fledged audio medium. However, with the growing popularity of podcasts, many podcasters have embraced video podcasting as a way to stand out and reach an even larger audience.

The video is extremely popular. Users are averaging 19 hours per week watching online videos in 2022, which is nearly 50% more than in 2018. So, podcast creators who want their show to see more growth and appeal to the widest audience are adding video elements to their podcasts.

What is the purpose of a podcast?

A podcast can have many purposes, but the main one is to entertain your audience. Podcast listeners may have one of several reasons for subscribing to a podcast, such as:

- Get updates on current events.
- Get to know a new topic or subject.
- Laugh at the co-hosts' jokes.
- Listen to interviews with popular or famous guests.
- Try an audio or narrative drama.

But behind each of these reasons is the desire to be entertained. Whether it's because they want to learn something new or simply have something to take their minds off a mundane task, listeners want to enjoy the experience of listening to a podcast.

If they don't like it, they probably won't come back.

3.1.4 Audiobooks.

Audiobooks are voice recordings of the text of a book that you listen to instead of reading. Audiobooks can be exact, word-for-word versions of books or abridged versions.

You can listen to audiobooks on any smartphone, tablet, computer, home speaker system, or in-car entertainment system.

Figure 13 - Audiobook – listen to a book.

Audiobooks are usually purchased and downloaded in the same way as music and digital video. They can also be purchased from online bookstores or downloaded for free from public domain websites.

Most public library systems offer audiobook downloads online – all you need is a library card. Even Spotify has an audiobook section.

Available as digital audio files, audiobooks can be played on a wide range of consumer electronic devices, including phones, tablets, and computers – any device that supports audio streaming.

When you buy or download audiobooks from the internet, they usually come in one of the following audio formats:

1. MP3.

   A file with the MP3 file extension is an MP3 audio file developed by Moving Pictures Experts Group (MPEG). The abbreviation stands for MPEG-1 or MPEG-2 Audio Layer III.

2. WMA.

   A file with the WMA file extension is a Windows Media Audio file. Microsoft created this format to compete with MP3, and it is often used for online music streaming.

3. AAC.

   AAC is short for Augmentative and Alternative Communication. Communication devices, systems, strategies, and tools that replace or support natural speech are known as augmentative and alternative communication (AAC).

   These tools help a person who has difficulty communicating using speech.

   The first "A" in AAC stands for Augmentative Communication. When you augment something, you add to it or complement it.

   Augmentative communication is when you add something to your speech (e.g., sign language, images, a card board). This can make your message clearer to your listener.

   The second "A" in AAC stands for Alternative Communication. That's when you can't speak. It's also when your speech isn't understood by others. In that case, you need a different way to communicate.

Most media devices are designed to play any of these file types.

Figure 14 – AAC has revolutionized access to digital content.

There are many websites and apps that provide access to audiobooks, both free and paid. Here are some of them:

1. Apple Books: Audiobooks for iOS and macOS devices are available for download in the app and in the Apple Books store.
2. Audible.com: While audiobooks can be purchased individually, Audible offers a monthly subscription service that provides one free audiobook download per month. Use the Audible app for Android or iOS to listen on mobile devices.
3. AllYouCanBooks.com: This website offers unlimited access to thousands of downloadable audiobooks. This paysite offers the first month for free.
4. Project Gutenberg: This website is known for offering thousands of free books in the public domain. Not as well known is its growing collection of human-read audiobooks that can be accessed over the internet.
5. Downpour: A commercial audiobook website that sells individual audiobooks, as well as a monthly subscription if you prefer.
6. Nook Audiobooks: Barnes & Noble's audiobook website sells a large collection of audiobooks.
7. OverDrive: An app that offers thousands of audiobooks from over 30,000 local libraries.

3.1.5 Subscription programs.

A subscription plan is a purchase option.

A subscription plan allows you to choose how often a product can be delivered. This is called "delivery frequency" For example, weekly delivery.

A subscription plan allows you to:

- Offer multiple delivery frequencies.
- Set up customer billing options.
- Choose the subscription discount (optional).
- Associate products with these subscription plans.

A subscription group can have a single subscription plan or multiple subscription plans (for example, weekly, monthly, and quarterly plans)

Sample subscription plan:

Nespresso sells subscriptions to its coffee.

One of the subscriptions caters to a group of customers called Ambassador.

In this group, he created three subscription plans.

Subscription Plan 1: "Weekly Delivery"

Subscription Plan 2: "Monthly Delivery"

Subscription Plan 3: "Quarterly Delivery"

Customers can choose the subscription options and receive different discounts.

3.1.6 Electronic magazines.

A digital magazine, also known as an electronic magazine or ezine, is very similar to its print version, but it is published in digital form instead of being printed on paper.

It can be read on a computer and allows a magazine to take advantage of digital technology and add animations and links within the magazine to make it more informative or aesthetically better.

The cost of printing is eliminated and the price of publishing is greatly reduced, so most digital magazines do not require the same amount of advertising as print magazines.

Some digital magazines come with a one-time printing license for those who prefer paper magazines, but this is not always true, and someone may inadvertently violate copyright law by printing ezine.

3.1.7 White Paper.

A white paper is an informational document issued by a business or non-profit organization to promote or highlight the capabilities of a solution, product, or service that it offers or plans to offer.

White papers are also used as a method of presenting government policies and legislation and assessing public opinion.

Main features:

1. A white paper provides compelling, factual evidence that a particular offering is a superior product or method for solving a problem.
2. White papers are commonly drafted for business-to-business marketing purposes between a manufacturer and a wholesaler, or between a wholesaler and a retailer.
3. White papers are sales and marketing documents used to attract or persuade potential customers to learn more about a particular product, service, technology, or methodology.
4. White papers are usually designed for business-to-business (B2B) marketing purposes between a manufacturer and a wholesaler, or between a wholesaler and a retailer. It can provide a detailed report or

guide on a specific product or topic, and is intended to educate your readers.
5. The facts presented in white papers are often backed up by research and statistics from reliable sources and may include charts, graphs, charts, tables, and other ways of visualizing data.
6. A white paper can communicate an organization's philosophy or present research findings related to an industry.

Types of white papers:

1. Backgrounders. They detail the technical characteristics of a new product or service. Designed to simplify complicated technical information, they are used to:
   - Support a technical assessment.
   - Launch a product.
   - Promote a product or industry leader.
2. Numbered lists. They highlight the key takeaways from a new product or service and are often formatted with titles and bullet points, such as the following familiar format:
   - 3 questions to ask.
   - 5 things you need to know.
   - 10 Tips.
3. Problem/solution documents. Identify specific problems faced by potential customers and suggest a data-driven argument for how a featured product or service provides a solution to:
   - Generate new sales.
   - Educate salespeople about product features.
   - Arouse the interest of the market.

3.1.8 Webinars.

The word 'webinar' is a mix of 'web' and 'seminar'. A webinar is an event held virtually that is watched exclusively by an online audience.

This differentiates it from a webcast, which also includes the presence of a physical audience. Other terms used as alternatives to webinar are web event, webinar, web lecture, and virtual event.

Figure 15 – How about a Webinar with Elon Musk?

Attendees follow the webinars via a PC, Mac, tablet or smartphone and can see and hear the speaker(s) thanks to audio and video feeds.

In addition to video footage, PowerPoint slides can be streamed in sync with the rest of the presentation. You can also use the screenshot functionality that allows you to show your viewers an app or website.

A webinar is a one-to-many form of communication: a presenter can reach a large, specific group of online viewers from a single location.

As long as it's used effectively, interaction during a webinar can be very powerful. Especially when you have a large number of participants, smart tools are essential to channel that interaction.

Thus, a webinar offers several interactive opportunities:

- Questions.
- Make small talk.
- Voting.
- Poll.
- Test.
- Call to action.
- Twitter.
- Growth of the webinar market.

'Less is more' – but that doesn't go for webinars. Defying all the latest communication trends to make everything shorter and faster, the average viewing time for webinars is increasing year after year and currently stands at 56 minutes!

The webinar market is also showing strong year-on-year growth. There are several reasons for this, not least because webinars are very effective. They also generate significant cost savings.

In addition, webinars are in-person, live, and interactive. From a pedagogical and educational point of view, webinars are interesting due to the high degree of interaction, helping participants to learn and understand more quickly.

3.1.9 Creation of infographics and templates.

According to the Oxford English Dictionary, an infographic (or information graphic) is "a visual representation of information or data."

But the meaning of an infographic is something much more specific.

The infographic is a visual piece widely used to present information, data, and concepts in an easy way, helping the reader understand when a content is of greater complexity.

They usually contain illustrations, texts, graphics, icons, and other media formats. Infographics are a valuable tool for visual communication.

The most creative and visually unique infographics are often the most effective because they hold our attention and don't let us go. But it's crucial to remember that the visuals in an infographic should do more than excite and engage.

3.2   How to become a digital producer?

To be a digital producer you need to be born with some talents. If you're not born with these talents, you'll need to develop them. The good news is that this is entirely possible.

For example, if you choose to be a producer of recorded or live classes, you need to be a charismatic teacher to earn money from this activity.

Figure 16 – Examples of digital products.

Not everyone has a charisma that conquers everyone. If you were born with this talent, it's easier to stand out, but you can develop teaching and exposing ideas techniques to fill any talent gaps.

In addition, to share knowledge through a digital course, it is essential to be an expert on the subject. The more mastery of the content you have, the more convincing your performance will be to your target audience.

To teach clearly, you often need to learn more about your chosen subject.

Knowing how to convey this content clearly and efficiently is also a talent that you need to have been born or have developed. A good option is to research and improve yourself until you are able to pass on this knowledge to others.

Realize then that self-knowledge, focus, and persistence will help you define the niche and devise efficient strategies. Even if you have an incredible and unprecedented idea, you will need to put it into practice.

The Internet is a very volatile and competitive medium. If you don't develop your authority in your chosen niche, you'll never see the result. Many professionals start with something small and, over time, gain space in the digital market.

Figure 17 – An online student. A sign of the times.

Note that most online courses and e-books seek to solve some problem. Some pain from your audience. Among these pains we can mention:

- ✓ Search for a better quality of life.
- ✓ Overcoming a financial crisis.
- ✓ Overcoming a phase of depression.
- ✓ To be successful and happy.

Another characteristic of a digital producer is to be entrepreneurial. The good thing is that this doesn't have to be a natural gift and can be developed from your desire to grow professionally.

A digital content creator needs to have an entrepreneurial spirit, because it is in the nature of this professional to be someone who innovates, creates something unprecedented that stands out for its quality and creativity. And it has as its raw material the observation of problems and the ability to propose the best way to solve them.

As an example, we can cite the situation in which you propose to improve the life of a person who cannot be successful, lives unemployed and without money.

Your job will be to produce relevant and really promising content for this person to have resulted in actions based on your product.

3.3 What are the best niches today?

You can produce products for any niche, but you should focus on topics that you master and that have the potential to sell on the Internet.

A good tip is to work on the issues where people come to you when they need help.

An example is the case of people who, despite not being famous chefs, understand everything about cooking and are always consulted by friends when they need culinary tips.

Cooking is a great niche, but don't be fooled. Just like you, there are many other people who also know all about recipes.

Once you've defined your niche, do some research and see what your future competition is doing.

After this analysis, think about more specific areas within the niche you have chosen and try to do what other people are not yet doing.

Continuing with the example of cooking, you realized that there is a lot of demand for recipes, but that there are also many online courses about it.

A good option, then, may be to create courses on food preparation for those who live alone. Another option might be to create courses for weekend cooks.

But always keep your eyes peeled for pitfalls:

- Don't be seduced by courses that promise easy money and little work as a digital producer.
- Success in any profession directly depends on the quality of your work.
- In the world of the Internet, the competition is unimaginable!

3.4 Be an authority and sell more

In order for your customers to trust your digital products, you need to be considered an authority. This can be achieved through a blog, a Youtube channel, or by producing content on social media.

Your videos, texts, audios and/or images need to have a good audience and must be aligned with the information products you will market.

It is necessary to always be present in digital media so that people feel close to you. Remember the maxim: those who are not seen are not remembered.

So, take the time to comment and like your audience's posts. It is these best practices that will help you become an authority on the subject you master and sales will be a natural consequence when you launch your product.

3.5 Advantages and disadvantages of being a digital producer

Advantages:

- Work based on the subjects you master.
- Produce products that you enjoy selling.
- The prospect of earnings is virtually limitless.
- Time flexibility, as you are your boss.
- Possibility to create products with very little investment and high return.
- The distribution of the product is done over the internet, without the high logistics costs with transportation and storage, among others.
- You can work from any part of the world.
- Possibility to implement a large network of affiliates to sell your products, paying only the commission for it.

Disadvantages.

- You can only make money from what you produce.
- The competition is very high.
- The unit price of the products is generally low. You have to sell a lot to gain scale.

3.6 Are there challenges to overcome?

There always is, isn't there. I have listed here the 3 challenges that I consider to be the main ones.

1. The first challenge is to take the necessary actions to maintain your lifestyle. That's why it's important to know:
    a. what you want to produce.
    b. what resources they have available today.
    c. what methods you should use to generate income.
2. The second challenge is to be able to maintain consistency in what you produce. Determine days of the week for each content to be published and maintain the level of interactions you have on your social networks.
3. The third challenge is to stay focused. Unlike other professions, you'll need to make an effort to produce on your own. The success and failure of your strategy is solely your responsibility.

3.7 How much does a digital producer make?

Instead of telling you numbers, I'm going to list some digital producers who earn fortunes.

This is the case of Rede Globo, Netflix, Warner Bros, universities, entertainment giants, bookstores, among many other corporations.

Talking about creating content is automatically linked to working on the Internet. Access to networks has done the work of democratizing access and access to content production.

The digital content market absorbs advertisers, video editors, fashion producers, athletes, salespeople, medical journalists, among other professionals who were trained to work on other fronts, but who were attracted by this professional segment.

Figure 18 – Make a lot of money. The dream possible.

Thus, the money you will earn is determined by you.

4 WAY 2 – MAKE MONEY AS A BLOGGER.

Nowadays, blogs are recognized as a long-term business model and in order to gain space, blogs need the skills of their administrators to be continuously improved and high traffic to be maintained.

In the beginning they were created to share opinions, artistic expressions or hobbies. Over time they have established themselves as a very practical way and an excellent idea of how to work and make money on the internet.

> *By learning and applying the right strategies, you can have a highly lucrative way of working.*

Today's technologies make room for new bloggers to be the next influencers of the digital age. Take the example of Youtubers, Instagramers and bloggers who have made and make their hobbies a profession.

Making money with blogs, Youtube and other channels is an increasingly common reality, which allows people to make a living from their passions.

Figure 19 – A Youtuber at work.

It is necessary to remember, however, that from the moment you decide to monetize your hobby, you become an entrepreneur, to a greater or lesser extent. And the fact of running a business requires a lot of work. Sometimes even more than a traditional job.

To pursue a career as a blogger you don't have to be a journalist, publicist or architect. Not even going to college or majoring. Just like to write, post photos, give your opinion or make reviews.

To help you, I'm going to teach you everything about the universe of bloggers and teach you what are the best strategies to make money blogging, becoming a digital entrepreneur.

Here are some tips for structuring your blog.

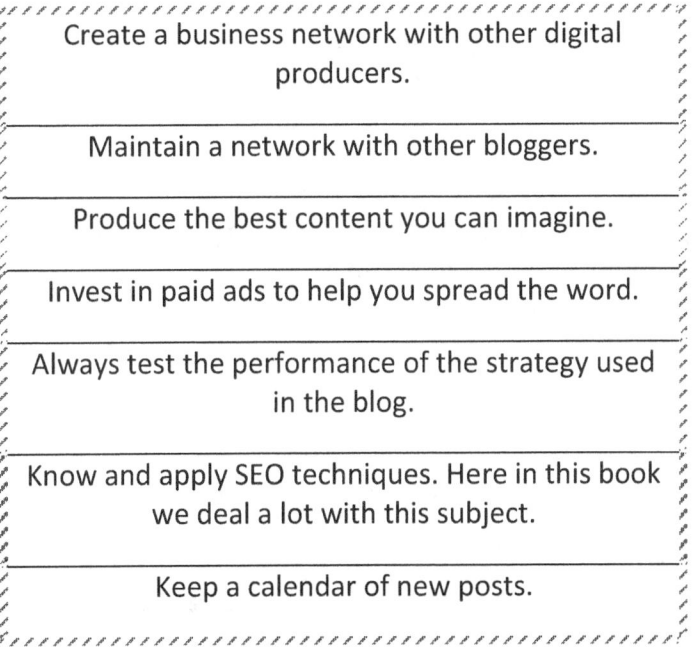

Figure 20 – How to structure a blog.

4.1   Ideas to make money blogging.

Currently we have many ways available to generate income with blogging.

By having your presence increased in the Internet world, you will become a reference in your niche. This is very useful for you to be able to provide consulting, advisory and mentoring services.

An interesting example is the case that you are a blogger who has vast knowledge of fashion and who treats the subject very confidently on your blog.

You can offer fashion consulting, visual production, mentoring for modeling agencies, and various guidance to your visitors.

With this type of work, it is possible to apply your knowledge on the subject and enhance word-of-mouth marketing based on the content of your blog.

And pay attention to this important tip:

> *Always ask your customers for testimonials about the service and post them prominently on your blog.*

The social proof generated by testimonials is a very efficient mental trigger and accelerates the generation of more credibility for future customers.

4.2 Sale of advertising.

Many bloggers make money by selling advertising space on their blogs to brands that want to advertise or merchandising.

If, in your case, you already have a certain authority and a good average of daily visitors, you can make a lot of money selling these spaces.

But don't try to "put the cart before the horse." Without having good numbers of daily visitors, you won't be able to attract the attention of companies and brands.

If you're in the early stages with your blog, you can look for brands and offer outreach in exchange for good counterparts.

But don't get carried away by the money of products that have no connection to your niche and that don't add value to your audience. This can jeopardize your credibility.

4.3 Make postings on your blog.

If you sell your own products, you can use the blog as an additional channel to launch your products.

Have a link to your sales page prominently displayed on your blog. This will make the buying process easier and take interested parties to a place where they will have more information about the product.

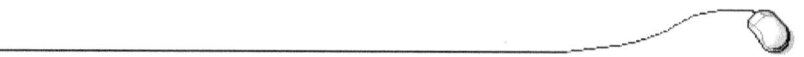

Also think about aligning this strategy with promotions or actions that lead your readers to feel benefited from a discount or a gift when buying the product.

And remember, the communication on the sales page should also be aligned with the content of your blog.

4.4   Add your opinion

An easy behavior to be observed in consumers of products sold on the Internet is that most have the habit of reading recommendations for a desired product before closing the purchase.

This is then a great way to sell digital products on your blog and gain the trust of your audience.

Writing recommendations and reviews about products that are in evidence and that you can analyze is a great way to sell advertising and the product itself.

In this case, you will do direct advertising and boost your authority through content marketing.

Here's another important tip.

> *The information needs to be complete and 100% true.*

A differential in your review may be that you offer a *test drive* of the product or negotiate this possibility with the manufacturer or manager of your affiliate program. This decreases the risk to the consumer and establishes a trust-based relationship with your readers.

The blog can also be used to promote lives or any other content that can provide more information to potential buyers and answer possible questions about the product.

4.5   Online courses and e-books.

Online courses are increasingly in demand, this is due to the ease of being accessed and consumed on any smartphone or computer from anywhere.

Your followers are feeling how technology is creating a world of opportunities and that they can learn new skills and accelerate their professional development with digital content.

Your blog can be formatted or transformed into content with richer, more complete and up-to-date material for those who want to learn about the subject you are dealing with.

You can create e-books or video courses and utilize the blog to turn your visitors into customers.

As an example, let's look at the case of a blog that deals with travel. How about creating e-books about free tourism options, family outings, restaurant tips or with the calendar of free visiting days in museums.

They can focus on a city, a country, or a travel style.

And here I've listed just a few possibilities. You have a whole universe of options to work with. Of course, all depending on how much you know about the subject.

Figure 21 – A student in an online course.

Online courses also have the advantage of you focusing on sales and scaling your earnings, as the content produced can generate several products.

With a low cost to produce the content you can have a high return on your initial investment without additional logistics costs and you can sell online to people who are everywhere in the world without language or customs limitations.

4.6 What about selling digital products?

Having a blog that has a loyal audience is a great differential to sell anything and this includes digital products.

It can be a product of your own, something sold in an affiliate program, or third-party products in exchange for commissions.

But I recommend that you take some precautions so that the promotion of the product is assertive and you can arouse the interest of your readers instead of scaring them away.

Respect the coherence between your blog's product and niche. This should be the golden rule of your ads. As with selling advertising, you should select digital products that are aligned with the topics you cover on your blog.

For example, if you write about sports, you should ideally promote videos, games, and e-books related to the sports world.

If your area of expertise is automotive launches, look for content about car factories, dealerships, workshops, and custom items for automobiles.

This coherence is important to generate empathy and engagement in the reader, as they perceive that indication as something you really recommend.

If you, like me, address different topics, it is best to be guided by the content that arouses the most interest in your audience and also by the most frequent questions in the comments.

Thus, you will have a better chance of selecting products that add value to your followers.

4.7   Strategies to make your endeavor easier.

You already know that to make money from your blog you will have to sell advertising, services or products. The more empathy and engagement your audience has with your blog, the more they will propagate your content.

It is essential to always offer correct informative content that educates and builds loyalty to your followers, answers their questions and creates a bond of trust and credibility so that there is a recurrence in visits and sales.

Below I will present you with strategies for you to start your blog and/or consolidate it as an excellent sales and income generation tool.

4.7.1   Choose your niche according to your goals and your knowledge.

You need to decide which segment of services and products you will be working with. Are you going to create e-books or online courses? Will you be an affiliate? Or will you offer consulting/mentoring services?

From this definition, your blog content should lead your customer to your product. Think about utilizing content marketing strategies to maximize your results.

The competition on the Internet is immense. To be able to win in this environment and make money, your main concern, when creating a blog, should be to produce quality content and always be guided by the subjects that are of interest to your followers.

Think about it, people will only be on your blog if they want to read what you write, see your photos, or know about your news. There is no other reason.

Being in tune with your audience is no easy feat. The younger you are, the faster your attention shifts, and the older you are, the harder it is to gain trust.

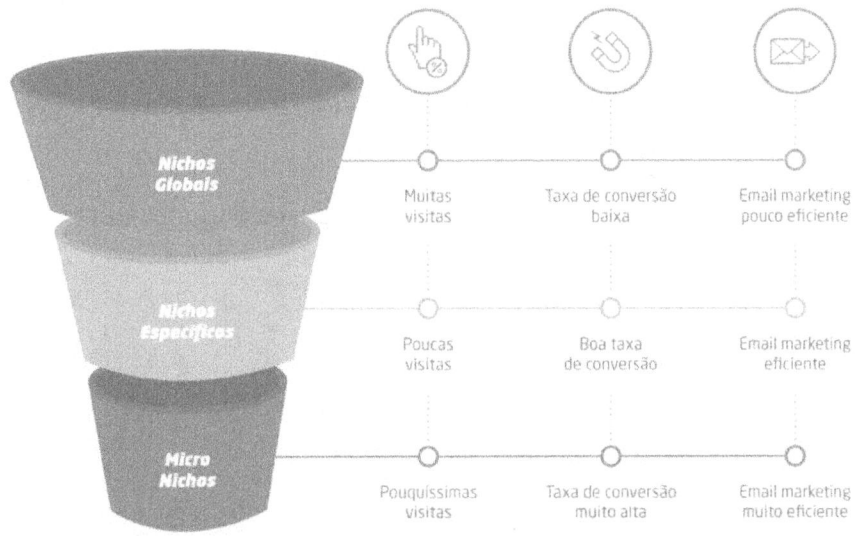

Figure 22 – The niche funnel.

There are several market analysis alternatives available on online platforms. Be in tune with what is being discussed the most at the moment, participate in social networks and search for the topics mentioned in the *trending topics*[4].

A good tool to stay up to date on what is being searched for the most on the Internet is Google Trends. It shows you what's being searched for the most at the moment and how much of an audience a particular subject has.

Keep track of your competitors' posts and foreign blogs. This can help you understand what's working with other blogs.

4.7.2 Be a cross-platform blogger

When thinking about creating a blog, it is common for its creator to be concerned only with written posts.

Even if your blog is about poetry or some more technical subject, the richer and more diverse your content is, the more interesting it will be.

---

[4] Trending topics (or TTs) are a list of topics most commented on by Twitter users at any given time. Through the tool, it is possible to know what is happening most important in the world.

Use a variety of formats, such as images, videos, audios, and infographics.

You can also maximize a post that has had the most hits or the most comments on derivative content that treats the subject in more detail and has more videos on the subject or has other infographics.

Don't forget to provoke your followers to participate in the discussions generated by your post.

4.7.3   Be a slave to your editorial calendar.

You may find this proposal unsympathetic, but rest assured that it is excellent advice.

One of the main conditions for your audience to be frequent on your blog is knowing that you have a content posting routine. An editorial calendar is an efficient tool for maintaining the frequency of posts you've put out.

\	Cronograma de postagens Semanais				
Segunda	Decoração	Fotos	Dicas	Quotes	Vídeos
Terça	Resenhas	Resenhas Duplas	R. Livros + Filme		
Quarta	Tags	Desafios	Maratonas	101 em 1001	Enquetes
Quinta	Resenhas	Resenhas Duplas	R. Livro + Filme		
Sexta	Entretenimento	Playlist	Whishlist	Dicas	Novidades
Sábado	Resenhas de Filmes	Falando sobre Séries	Escola / Faculdade		
Domingo	Parcerias	Sorteios	Promoções	Caixinha de correio	Avisos

Figure 23 – Example of a legendary editorial.

For example, you should post new content three times a week. Disclose this calendar and meet this deadline without missing a day.

By doing so, you will have formalized a virtual contract between you and your followers, who will know when the blog will have news and will be able to participate by commenting on the content.

A good alternative to not getting caught in the traps of parties or special dates is to produce the posts and leave them scheduled. Most blogging platforms allow you to schedule posts to be published. If there's a problem with your availability to post on a day, you'll remain impeccable with your calendar.

4.7.4 Have a consolidated network.

By creating an email list in which your followers or visitors can register, you will enable a tool with great potential to generate more traffic to your website, to promote digital products, to participate in your lives and product launches.

This list can be a great channel for promoting digital product launches, partnerships, and promotions, directly on your reader's screen, even if they haven't visited your website.

The conversion cycle from visit to sale can be understood in the following steps:

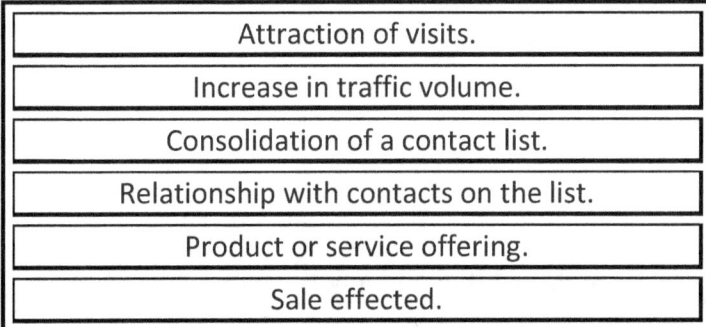

Figure 24 – Conversion cycle.

Worry about the segmentation of your contacts so that when you make use of the list for communications, it is targeted and delivers content that is relevant to that recipient.

Avoid being inconvenient, invasive, or excessive. There are several automation tools that allow you to select contacts based on their navigation and interactions on your page.

The following figure summarizes good initiatives to have a list of all your visitors.

Free content.	Offer current and complete materials for free and ask for users' email in return.
Forms	Make contact forms available on your blog and ask them to fill them out to participate in promotions.
Newsletter	You can produce exclusive content for the subscribers on the list. They will feel privileged to receive exclusive content or before others.
Webinars	If you have good traffic on your blog, you can promote *webinars* to discuss the most requested topics or promote products by requesting email as an entrance ticket to events.

Figure 25 – Good initiatives to have a list of your visitors.

4.7.5 Partner with other bloggers.

Strengthen your internet presence by partnering with other bloggers who are not your direct competitors but are still part of the same market.

You can have spaces on the blog for guest posts. In addition to the guest posting content that adds to your content, they will feel indebted and offer you space on their blog.

This type of action has the possibility of reaching a new portion of the target audience that is also interested in your content.

4.7.6 Build engagement on social media.

A blogger who values his profession has a constant presence on various social networks, producing exclusive content and strengthening the engagement of his audience.

But don't waste energy. Always look at which social networks your visitors use.

And pay attention to the characteristics of each social network. Each one has its own format, its own jargon, its memes, its own ideas. It is you who must adapt to them and not the other way around. Only then will you be able to deliver content that the audience can be interested in.

4.7.7 Learn SEO techniques – it makes all the difference.

SEO is the acronym *for Search Engine Optimization*. Translating from English it is "Search Engine Optimization".

SEO techniques, when used well, make your blog better positioned in search engine rankings.

This means that when someone does a search on Google or Internet Explorer, your blog will be present in the first results.

"Being better positioned in search results" translates into an increase in your organic traffic.

Organic traffic is that visit that comes to your blog for free.

If you appear in the first search results for terms that have a connection to your content, you will naturally have more recognition and will be able to take advantage of this interaction to attract buyers to your blog or to make sales.

The profession of SEO manager is one of the 19 ways to make money on the Internet covered in this book. It's worth taking a look at the chapter and maybe it's a second profession option for you.

4.7.8 Invest in paid traffic.

You're not the only entrepreneur who panics when they hear about paid ads. Even more so in a book like this that says all the time that it is possible to be an Internet professional with very low investment.

That's that! But the point here is for you to understand that paying for the ad is not an expense. It's an investment. It will generate traffic to your blog.

And you can use the ad to promote your product, the affiliate program product, or a launch. This is all against the backdrop of generating engagement for your blog.

Making money blogging, organically, can require patience and time to see results, which you may not have. That's why you have the option of resorting to paid ads and attracting visibility to your blog.

4.7.9 Know how to analyze performance indexes.

To understand what the result of your strategies is, it is necessary to analyze, measure, compare indices and then make adjustments and changes in route. One of the platforms I recommend is Analytics. It is very complex, but the time invested in it brings excellent results.

Another tool that will help you a lot is Google Search Console. It will help you analyze the keywords you want to use in your posts. From the positions they have been achieving in search engine results, you will be able to decide which keyword can rank your content better in user searches.

4.7.10 Be an eternal perfectionist.

This is not author paranoia, no. No catchphrase to attract their attention.

What I mean is that you need to be constantly analyzing and perfecting your blog all the time, always.

It's a good thing to A/B test your blog. These tests are done by making comparisons between marketing variables, with the aim of defining which variable generates the best responses in your case.

It's a little tricky, but over time you get used to the tasks to perform this test.

For example, you can test two *landing page* formats to determine which one will generate the highest conversion rate. This will help you customize the conversion buttons (CTA), change text and images, identify changes that generated more or less results, and change the frequency of email delivery.

I recommend that you research how to take these tests and incorporate them into your activities.

4.8 Advantages and disadvantages of being a blogger

Disadvantages

The blogger always needs to separate his professional activity from his private life.

When you mix personal and professional life, it's normal for personal life to become an eternal Instagram. Everything becomes character, fiction and staging. There's no way this will result in anything positive for the blogger as a human being.

Figure 26 - Blogging for a living can be difficult.

You may be slow to make money, or you may be deluded by periods of plenty and not plan for hard times.

It is necessary for you to have a lot of discipline to deal with personal finances in an unpredictable condition like the internet market.

And get this:

- Being a public figure isn't easy.
- You lose the right to your privacy.
- Your followers feel entitled to have their say and interfere in your life.
- There is a lack of recognition

- The profession does not exist.
- The blogger is seen as a tourist in the journalistic world.
- The fame that it yields a lot makes every kind of smart guy try to be a blogger.
- Since nothing is required for a person to be a blogger, it is difficult to separate the wheat from the chaff.

Advantages:

- Teach someone something.
- The satisfaction when you realize that you are teaching someone something.
- This learning relationship will bring you closer to your follower and will generate a very healthy collaboration context.
- Loving relationship with your followers
- Followers tend to respect and love their bloggers. It's great to have this affection from your audience.
- Be a manager of your work.
- You can work from home or wherever you wish.
- You make your work schedule.
- You set your goals and your timeline.
- Everyone can be a blogger.
- That's it. Anyone, of any age, ethnicity, gender, education level, or language can have a blog.
- Compatibility with other activities
- As you are a manager of your time, being a blogger does not compete directly with other activities.
- You can study or have another job without any problems.

5 WAY 3 – EARN MONEY AS A VIRTUAL ASSISTANT.

Do you understand administrative routines, are you proactive, and do you have the ability to talk on the phone?

So, becoming a Virtual Assistant can be a great way to make money on the internet, being able to work from home and have extra income.

Figure 27 – Virtual assistant is the profession of the moment.

There are dozens of self-employed professionals such as dentists, doctors, and engineers who work alone and accumulate many tasks ancillary to their profession, such as doing financial control, paying bills, answering emails, scheduling meetings, issuing invoices, and other various tasks.

Usually these professionals have a very high hourly rate, and it becomes more profitable to hire someone to perform these tasks, and with that come opportunities to work as a Virtual Assistant.

To work as a Virtual Assistant, you can access freelancer hiring platforms such as 99Freelas, Workana, and Freelancer.

In addition, it is important to enter into a service contract between you and the client to record the value set for the execution of the work, activities, time, and others.

This is a way to ensure transparency and security for both parties.

In case you want to know, there are some courses on the market that teach you how to work as a Virtual Assistant.

> *A virtual assistant is a self-employed professional who provides services to microentrepreneurs and professionals.*

You can perform services such as:

1. Customer service.
2. E-mail management.
3. Collection of delinquents.
4. Aftermarket.
5. Financial services.
6. Follow-up.
7. Issuance of invoice.
8. Scheduling appointments.
9. Calendar and schedule management.
10. Travel arrangements.
11. Organization of files and documents.
12. Monitoring and organization of e-mails.
13. Answer and direct calls.
14. Billing and accounting activities.
15. Write and keep records.
16. Evaluate potential customers, projects, partnerships, etc.
17. Maintain or update a client's social media or professional profile.

In short, anything that can be done over the phone or over the internet.

Even if you don't do it at first, you need to be an MEI (individual microentrepreneur) for the following reasons:

- To issue an invoice.
- To have a security in the event of an accident or for retirement.
- To make it clear to the client that there is no employment relationship.

What do you need to get started as a virtual assistant?

- Computer or laptop.
- Planner, pens, notepads.
- Internet access.
- Telephone.
- Professional email.
- WhatsApp.

Who hires virtual assistants?

- Doctors.
- Dentists.
- Lawyers.
- Photographers.

These are just a few of the professionals who hire virtual assistants. There are several others who need the help of a virtual assistant to help with their chores.

How to get your first customer:

- Talk to everyone around you, usually your first client is someone you know or referred by someone who knows your work.
- Go to places where people in your niche are, such as entrepreneur meetings, lectures, seminars, etc.
- Make a paper business card and leave it with people who can be your future customers, when they need it they will have your contact.

What is the salary of Virtual Assistant[5]?

The national average salary for a Virtual Assistant is R$1,551 in Brazil.

---

[5] Value as of October 2022. This salary estimate is based on the 54 salaries submitted anonymously to Glassdoor by employees with the position of Virtual Assistant.

6 WAY 4 - MAKE MONEY AS A VIDEO EDITOR

One of the highest-paid professions in Audiovisual, the Video Editor is in charge of editing and other post-production aspects, such as color treatment and assembling soundtracks.

It receives all the raw material (videos, photos or audios) and delivers the finished and edited material.

Figure 28 – Well-done video editing is a big challenge.

The portfolio is critical for the video editor. Try to show your most outstanding works, while choosing a platform that values the visualization of your productions.

Editing software is constantly updated, with increasingly powerful and efficient tools.

Knowing them helps you increase your productivity and avoid losing more specific jobs. The most well-known software is Adobe Premiere, Sony Vegas, and Movie Maker.

6.1 Is it better to be a video editor with a steady job or a freelancer?

Each has its advantages and disadvantages. The freelancer has greater freedom in terms of choosing jobs, with the opportunity to do everything at home, while the fixed has to meet schedules.

Although the income of the fixed professional is not variable, the freelancer can end up earning higher prizes and still have greater control over the work he would like to be involved in.

However, being an editor is not as simple as it seems, because in addition to these attributions, he must use a lot of creativity and set up storytelling so that the content makes sense to the target audience.

In this way, you as a professional video editor should leave the material in the best possible way, based on the purpose of this material.

That's why a video editor must participate from the planning to the elaboration of the product so that it captures the essence of the project.

6.2 Where to work?

My recommendation in this text is for the internet-based work, doing video marketing to promote your own products or even your professional/personal image.

In addition, as an editor you can also work on:

- Marketing agencies.
- Visual content agencies.
- Game creation companies.
- Youtube channels.
- Institutional communication.
- Cinema.
- Television channels.
- Graphic animation companies.

Thus, working with video editing is also a good opportunity for you who want to undertake and earn money on the internet with games, distance education, Youtube channels or also in cinema and television.

6.3 Training and salary.

A good video editor must have some specific skills and master the use of some editing software, such as:

- Final Cut.
- Adobe Premiere.
- After Effects.
- Sony Vegas.

Although there are specific trainings for video editors, they are usually not required.

Proving that you have knowledge in this area by doing an excellent job, even if you have a degree in another area, you are already well recognized to win a job.

However, knowledge is never too much and the video editing market is looking for qualified people to give the correct direction to the workflow to be requested.

So, always try to train yourself, learn new editing techniques, create your portfolio with your best work, be aware of trends and it is always good to be an expert in some area.

The salary of a video editor varies according to the region, size of the company, experience, working hours, training, and other factors, but the average salary for a professional in this area is R$ 2,000.00 according to Talent in October 2022.

7 WAY 5 – EARN MONEY WITH AFFILIATE PROGRAM.

One of the marketing effects of the growth of the internet as an e-commerce tool was to enhance the provision of segmented and selected services according to consumer preferences.

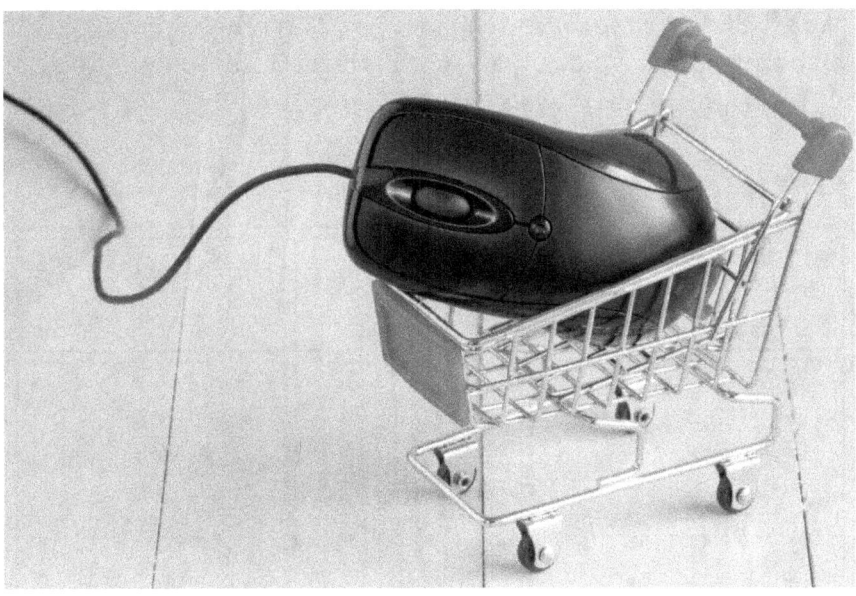

Figure 29 – The mouse is the buying tool.

The Affiliate Program is one of those cases in which technology has created means for a segment that operated offering products door-to-door to be extended to the customer's personal computer or to be available in the palm of their hand, in mobile applications.

Affiliate programs emerged from the popularization of blogging and thrived with influencers. In the beginning, advertisers looked for bloggers according to their niche to establish a partnership.

The relationship was simple, based on the testimony of bloggers. They received commissions for talking directly about the product in their posts or associating them with their personal brand.

Hence we have the initial basis of how affiliate programs work. The higher the consumer's degree of trust with the blogger, the greater the chance of buying the product they recommended.

The affiliate program has grown a lot and is currently based on major digital influencers, content producers from Youtube[6], Instagram[7] and Tik Tok[8], gamers[9], celebrities and even characters from the virtual world.

7.1 How does it work?

Joining an affiliate program is very simple. All you have to do is sign up for one of the platforms that have this sales model and choose from the thousands of physical and digital products available to advertise and sell.

You need to have	You need to choose	It is necessary to
❖ Over 18 years. ❖ A valid email address. ❖ A computer. ❖ A wi-fi connection.	One or more affiliate programs.	Formalize your participation in the chosen affiliate program by creating an account on the platform.

Figure 30 – Criteria for participation in an affiliate program.

---

[6] YouTube is an online platform that allows the creation and consumption of video content via streaming. That is, to watch the published videos, it is not necessary to download any type, you just need to be connected to the internet.

[7] Instagram is a visual, creative and interactive social network. It makes it possible to share images and short videos directly from the mobile application. In it, it is also possible to follow users, like, comment and share publications.

[8] TikTok is a social network for sharing short videos, of 15 or 60 seconds and 3 minutes, but it offers extensive resources to edit them. You can include filters, subtitles, soundtrack, gifs, make cuts, and get creative.

[9] Gamer is the name currently given to the famous "video game players". These can be both professional gamers and free-time gamers.

Be aware of the particularities and differentials of the program you choose.

An important detail, and one that interests us a lot, is the commission percentage. The usual are commissions of 3 to 7% for physical products and 40 to 70% for digital products.

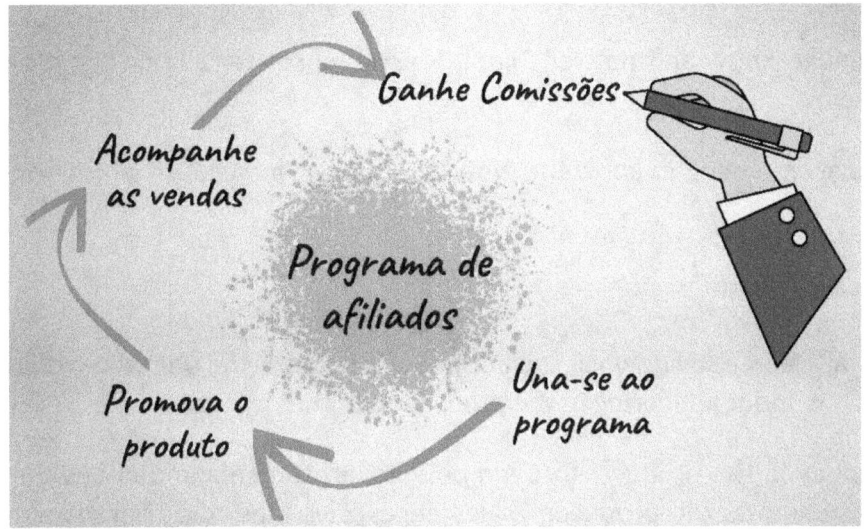

Figure 31 – Percentage of commissions.

The affiliate, which is you, associates with a platform for selling products on the Internet. You receive affiliate designation because you join a program, choose the products you want to sell, define your marketing strategy, advertise your offers, make the sale, and receive money for your work.

You will receive a unique link to the sales platform so that your sales can be identified. It is possible to be an affiliate of physical and digital products, courses, and services.

A supplier, which can be a manufacturer, is an importer, wholesaler, or distributor, makes its product available to sell on a platform that is available so that affiliates can execute sell by receiving commissions.

If you choose to work with sales promotion of physical products there are excellent companies with affiliate programs, such as Amazon, Americanas, Magazine Luiza, eBay, Hostinger and Shopify.

If you want to work only with digital products and don't have to worry about keeping track of physical delivery and inventory from large retailers, you can analyze alternatives that deal with digital products on sites like Hotmart, Eduzz, and Monetizze.

But pay attention!

It is important to know and master Digital Marketing strategies and tools to boost your sales.

But before that, you need to know the types of affiliates and choose which one you fit into.

7.1.1 Investor affiliate.

The investor affiliate, also known as the arbitrator affiliate, is the one who works anonymously, without appearing in the promotion of the products.

It invests money in the products through paid advertisements and drives the reached consumers to the producers' sales pages. This type of affiliate is not responsible for generating any relationship between the product and its image.

As you may have already noticed, the differential of this modality is that it can operate in several niches and sell several different products.

Investments tend to produce results faster and on a larger scale, but note that in order to keep sales flowing and earn steady income, you need to maintain investments in ads and campaigns.

The initial investment is up to you, but the return is proportional to the amount invested. Small investments tend to result in small results. But be careful. Larger investments don't necessarily result in great results.

It is essential to:

- Know how to advertise on the main ad platforms, such as Face-book Ads[10] and Google Ads[11].
- Learn how to analyze campaign results.
- Measure return on investment (ROI).
- Know basic design to create good images to use in your ads.
- Be a good copywriter[12].
- Have a lot of patience.

If you consider that you may have a future as an affiliate investor, choose your product and master the best paid traffic strategies to make a lot of money.

7.1.2 Authority affiliate.

Unlike the investor affiliate, the authority affiliate associates the product with their knowledge, produces relevant content for their persona and uses social networks to take the consumer to the product platform.

The authority affiliate is a modern sales representative.

To create your content, you must study your target audience and discover their interests, desires, goals, and difficulties. The more in-depth and detailed this study is, the better your chances of pleasing it.

It's also necessary to figure out what social network or media your prospect uses. Whether it's to find answers to your doubts and questions or just for entertainment. You see, there is no doubt that it is on this platform that you should position yourself as an expert on the subject of your product.

To succeed as an authority affiliate it is important to master:

---

[10] It is Facebook's paid media system that offers a wide variety of ad formats. Through it, it is possible to create campaigns and strategies to promote your brand on Facebook and Instagram.
[11] Google Ads (formerly Google AdWords) is Google's ad platform. Its first version was released in 2000 and since then it has led the Online Media market. Through Google Ads it is possible to create Search ads, Display ads, on Youtube, Gmail and the Play Store.
[12] Copywriting is the process of producing persuasive texts for Marketing and Sales actions, such as the content of emails, websites, catalogs, advertisements and sales letters, for example. The professional responsible for developing the text (also called copy) is known as a Copywriter.

1. Persuasion techniques to try to lead your audience to make the decisions indicated by you.
2. Mental triggers that are, in general, subtle or even subliminal ways of manipulating questions and phrases that aim to persuade the customer to follow your opinion.
3. Copywriting, which is the production of texts that work on persuasion to generate sales.
4. Storytelling[13] which is the good old art of telling stories to convey a message that also aims to generate sales.
5. Communication skills to know how to deal with different audiences.
6. Putting together content guidelines to organize thoughts and perform better as a *copywriter* and *storyteller*.
7. Keyword research and ranking to enhance the recovery of your content in searches.

If you have mastery over a subject or are interested in working as an authority affiliate, search for products in your chosen niche, start producing valuable content, and build your authority.

Rest assured that by following all this that I have guided you will have all the necessary skills and techniques to recommend products or services that solve problems of your potential customers and make a lot of money on the internet with the sales made.

---

[13] Storytelling is an English term. "Story" means story and "telling" means to tell. More than a mere narrative, Storytelling is the art of storytelling using techniques inspired by screenwriters and writers to convey a message in an unforgettable way.

7.2   Positives and Negatives of Affiliate Programs

Figure 32 – It is very important to evaluate positive and negative points.

7.2.1   Positives – go in faith!

The initial investment is low.

- ✓ This is a really cost-effective way to start an internet business.
- ✓ Affiliate programs are free of charge.
- ✓ Your cost will be related to the forms of disclosure you adopt.

There is no inventory involved in the selling process.

- ✓ Inventory and deliveries are managed by the affiliate program company.
- ✓ No logistical problems

You don't have to create products

- ✓ On an affiliate platform, there are a multitude of good products for you to broker sales.
- ✓ There is no need to waste time and effort acquiring knowledge, recording, editing, and investing time and money to develop a product.

The products have the quality selected by you.

- ✓ We know that there are many low-quality products on the market, but you have complete freedom to inform yourself and can select the quality and niche of products you want to represent.
- ✓ It is entirely possible to represent a quality product immediately.

The money comes to you quickly as sales can be made from the first moment of affiliation due to the ease of joining the programs.

Freedom to work.

- ✓ You can join various affiliate programs.
- ✓ You can work with a program for each type of product.

Figure 33- The trophy is your income.

7.2.2 Negatives – open your eyes!

You are rewarding only on the first sale.

- ✓ The reward only occurs on the initial sale.
- ✓ You don't earn again if your customer later buys another product from the same seller, or renews access to a course or service you referred.
- ✓ You only invoice in relation to the product you sold.

It takes time to build your clientele, and it takes a lot of effort and dedication to activate your sales cycle.

You have no control over the delivery of the products

- ✓ This can lead to complaints that may reach you.
- ✓ When you complain on the product platform, you will be served as an affiliate of the program. Their priority is the same as that of all other affiliates.

The market is very competitive. You need to work differently to stand out and win over customers.

There are no earnings per referral spread. When your customer refers the product or service to someone else, you don't get paid anything for selling that other person.

There is no sustainability. Everything you sell in a month doesn't generate sequential or future results. Next month you need to work on sales as if you had never sold anything.

7.3 What now? Which program to choose?

Now that you know the main features of this way of making money on the Internet, you can analyze the factors – commission rates, product quality, and relevance to your niche.

To help you out, here are the main points of some of the top affiliate programs:

- Amazon Associates. One of the largest affiliate networks that offers commission rates of up to 20%.
- ConvertKit Affiliate Program – very easy joining process.
- Hotmart. Commissions are determined by the producers.
- eBay Partner Network. Vast collection of products and low redemption limit for your commissions.
- HubSpot's Affiliate Program. Altas comissões.
- SemRush Affiliate Program. Easy and quick to register, it offers tracking tools, analytical reports and high commissions.
- Hostinger Affiliate Program. Easy registration, provides sales monitoring tools, analytical reports and good commissions.
- ThirstyAffiliates. Redemption with no minimum limit.
- Amazon Associates. Multiple rewards programs and vast collection of products.
- Shopify Affiliates, You earn commission for every referral who creates a Shopify account using your referral link.
- ClickBank Affiliate. Instant affiliate link creation and wide range of commission rates
- WP Engine Affiliate. High commission rate and customized landing pages for promotions.

Choosing between affiliate programs can take a lot of analysis, but it's worth investing in the knowledge to support your choice.

8 WAY 6 – MAKE MONEY AS AN ONLINE FREELANCER.

If you are a copywriter, translator, designer, programmer, speak another language or so many other alternatives you can use this way to make money on the internet by being a freelancer.

Figure 34 – The happiness of the Freelancer: delivering the work.

A freelancer is a professional who works autonomously providing services to companies or people for certain periods. And when these jobs are done exclusively through the internet, they are called an online freelancer.

Unlike a traditional worker, the freelancer does not have any employment relationship with the company or person who hires their services.

As a result, service contracts have a determined duration, according to the professional's availability and the client's demand. Even so, the employment relationship can be recurring if both parties are interested.

And since the freelancer does not have any employment relationship, he can work serving several clients at the same time.

There are several websites that specialize in bringing together Freelancers and people interested in various services, and the demand is very high. That is, there will always be services for the freelancer.

All you have to do is register on these sites, such as Workana, and offer your services.

You can also provide consulting services if you are an expert in any area, such as fashion, finance, personal development, marketing, etc.

Providing services as a freelancer is one of the most lucrative ways that exist today, as well as being a great alternative for those who want to work from home and leave the conventional work method.

And, if you know how to use digital marketing tools, you will be able to offer your freelancing services to people from anywhere in the country or the world.

Those who have already learned how to make money on the internet recommend that new entrepreneurs start by freelancing, as it is one of the fastest ways to get a financial return.

8.1 How to succeed as a freelancer?

Even though most freelancing professions don't have that many requirements, in all of them you need to develop skills that will make you an outstanding professional and able to make a lot of money.

Here are some of these skills:

- Be highly productive to deliver the jobs within the deadline set by the client;
- Learn faster and better everything that happens in your market and the best technologies to perform your activities;
- Know how to plan financially;
- Know how to organize your tasks and prioritize the most important ones;
- Be a good salesperson to offer your services and demonstrate high value in front of your customers;
- Have the agility to prepare proposals within the freelancing platforms.

8.2 Is it necessary to have a college degree to work as a freelancer?

According to the Mercado Freelancer 2018 survey, conducted by Rock Content, We Do Logos and 99jobs, more than 90% of Brazilian freelancers have higher education (undergraduate or graduate).

Despite this, the requirement for a degree to work as an online freelancer depends on the field. For those in which professional practice requires a specific training, such as architecture, engineering or accounting, a degree may be required.

In others, where the diploma is not a legal requirement, the market itself asks for specialized professionals, such as journalism and marketing. In these niches, freelancers without a degree end up lagging behind competitors.

In creative pursuits, such as photography, graphic design, and video editing, on the other hand, the talent and experience of the professional count for much more than the degree.

8.3 Advantages and disadvantages.

If the number of professionals entering this market every year continues to grow, it must be worth it.

In fact, working as a freelancer brings a number of advantages to the professional.

And you can check out some of them below:

- More flexibility: The biggest benefit of being a freelancer is the flexibility that this type of work provides. Depending on the type of activity, the self-employed professional can make their own schedule and work from wherever they want (at home, in a library or on the beach).
- Possibility of earning more: In formal employment, no matter the workload, the salary will always be the same. As a freelancer, you're the one who determines how much you get paid per hour or completed work. In other words, the more demands delivered, the more money!
- Working with what you like: In a traditional job, it's common to participate in projects that we don't identify with. A freelancer, on the

other hand, has complete autonomy to accept the proposals they find most interesting.

And the disadvantages?

Obviously, not everything is rosy in the world of online freelancers and this type of work also has some drawbacks.

So, if you intend to enter this market, you can't help but evaluate the negative points.

- Poor stability: Despite being able to earn more compared to a formal job, a freelancer suffers from a lack of financial stability. It may be that, in certain periods, fewer jobs appear and the money is smaller. In other words, if you want to enter this market, you need to know how to deal with this uncertainty.
- No labor benefits: Another negative point is that, by choosing to work as a freelancer, you are giving up a series of rights guaranteed to formal workers. This includes 13th salary, paid vacations, FGTS and sick pay.

8.4   How to Get a Freelance Job.

To get jobs and make good money as a freelancer, you first need to define a niche market to work in (your specialty).

Then, just create your profile on an online platform of your choice and build a portfolio to promote your main works.

To be seen as a responsible professional, ask your clients for references and register them in your profile. Few ads are more effective than an old customer, aren't they? After all, those who have already hired your service and were satisfied have a great chance of speaking well of you and proving your commitment to what you do.

Even more important than knowing how to ask for referrals is always offering your best. Thus, you begin to be referred spontaneously, as you will have gained people's trust and shown that you are prepared to take on challenges.

Do your personal marketing. You need to create your brand, promote your work, and show what sets you apart from other freelancers, so that people conclude that you are the right professional for what they need.

To do this personal marketing assertively, find out your strengths and weaknesses and also know your competition. Thus, you will be able to build an attractive brand for customers and show that you offer exclusive and relevant advantages.

It is also important to know how to create partnerships and participate in events, forums and communities about the niche in which you operate, so that people start to get to know you and, especially, to discover your work.

Pay attention, then. To have good personal marketing:

- Have a website talking about yourself, your strengths and projects you have accomplished.
- Place customer testimonials on your website.
- Be active on social media, subtly mentioning what you do whenever possible.
- Value your work, don't charge too cheap.
- Stay friends with your good customers. This way you will be more recommended.
- Have a unique space to work.
- Be careful with the balance between work and play.
- Don't be sorry to dismiss 'suitcase' customers.
- Upgrade so the competition doesn't leave you behind.

8.4.1 Jobs of a freelancer.

Among the various products of a freelancer you can have as products:

- Create websites.
- Make banners.
- Edit videos.
- Translate texts.
- Produce articles.
- Set up online stores.
- Program.

- Optimization and SEO.
- Produce content for fanpages.

Next, check out some sites that you can sign up for and start earning money as a freelancer:

- Workana;
- 99 freelancers;
- Upwork;
- Fiverr;
- Guru;
- GetNinjas;
- General Communication;
- Prolancer;
- Nearjob;
- Freelancer.

8.5   What is the ideal platform?

There is no option that is ideal on what to do to make money on the internet, analyze if there is a vacancy for your profile and area of expertise, if not, try the next one, don't waste time.

If the platform has been around for a while, this is an indication that it works. In other words, you're likely to find jobs.

Figure 35 - The freelancer's question: which platform to choose?

Which platform is better: national or international? This is very important! However, there is no right or wrong answer. It's simple, if you want to apply for international vacancies, opt for an international platform. On the other hand, if you are starting and want to take your first steps, opt for something local, in the Brazilian scenario.

Test the platform, that's the golden rule! Choose two of the ones you liked the most and pay attention to making a quality registration, publish your profile and search for opportunities.

8.6 Don't wait for your chances to fall from the sky.

At some point, jobs will come up and when they do, grab the opportunity! It is possible that in the beginning you need to lower your initial value, while maintaining a fair value so as not to devalue your service and the market.

In your first jobs, you will be building a reputation and a portfolio so that you can later charge higher and higher values that are consistent with your skills.

9 WAY 7 – MAKE MONEY WITH AUDIO BOOK NARRATION.

Do you like to read books a lot? Do you have a pleasant voice? Do you have good diction?

Then you can use this way to make money on the internet.

You have the main tools you need to make money on the internet by narrating audio books.

More and more book authors are making their works available in audio book format. This is because the demand is increasing, as people are always in a hurry and prefer to listen to a book while driving, exercising, cooking, or doing any other activity that makes it impossible to stop to read.

There are platforms that you can sign up for and find this service. These platforms connect book authors with narrators.

To get a job, you can create a type of portfolio, with short audios of your voice narrating excerpts from books.

9.1 Take this case.

Actress Joana Caetano had not realized the potential of her voice, until a theater director called her attention to it and recommended her to do a job in the audiobook market.

Joana recorded The Diary of Anne Frank, the account of the Jewish girl written during World War II, between June 1942 and August 1944

"I already knew the book, but it's very different when it comes to narrating. Since it's a diary, the reading can't exactly be interpretive.

It's Anne talking about herself. And it was necessary to convey the anguish that she and her family were experiencing, trying to hide from the Nazis," he says. The recording of the 352 pages took a month and a half, and the pronunciation of names and expressions in German received special attention.

"I had to practice that a lot, because it wouldn't sound good to pronounce something wrong," says the narrator.

Although the work requires technique and discipline, the narrator is not exempt from being moved by the book, which is another aspect to be managed. "There were moments when I really had to take a break to breathe and regain concentration," says Joana.

9.2   Paulo Betti.

Experienced on stage, on film sets and in TV studios, actor Paulo Betti has been lending his voice to works such as the trilogy by writer Laurentino Gomes on the history of Brazil (1808, 1822 and 1889) for some time now. "I took everything from my experience as an actor into the narration," Betti says. "It's a tough job and I can't do more than three hours a session because it requires a lot of concentration. I have to interpret the text the first time, making the idea reach the listener.

To divide and pronounce the words well, I have to understand what I'm reading, otherwise the listener doesn't care", describes the actor, who points out the exact tone of the reading as the biggest challenge. "How do you say those words? Solemnly? Colloquial? What is the tone of each book, of each page, of each chapter, of each sentence? But it's all fascinating."

Paulo Betti also emphasizes the learning aspect related to this activity. "The history of Brazil is so rich and surprising. Sometimes I was stunned by what I was reading. I learned a lot," says the actor.

The selection of audiobook narrators has to be judicious, because each publication requires a type of voice and narration. "There are books that ask for something more formal; others, looser.

There are stories that look better with a female or more mature voice. Others ask for a more didactic and journalistic reading. And there are still stories that have resources such as sound," says Marta Ramalhete.

The process of producing an audiobook also involves a proofreader of the narration, who checks if the text was spoken correctly, if there are any pronunciation errors or exaggerated accent.

"The text that the narrator reads is exactly what is in the book; There is no adaptation. For this reason, everything that causes strangeness in the reader cannot enter. Hence the importance of the proofreader.

The reader has to immerse themselves in the story; You can't stop and think about the narrator," says the production manager. She states that the key word, when it comes to audiobooks, is credibility. "Regardless of whether it's fiction or not, the narrator must embody the author, his ideas. Nothing can sound fake."

9.3   Course.

It was because of noticing an expanding market that Marta Esteves and the voice actor, announcer, teacher and audiobook narrator Flávio Carpes created a course in June 2022 to qualify audiobook professionals.

In October 2022, they promoted another edition of the course, which is taught on two Saturdays, with 16 hours in total. Flávio Carpes has been working in the voice-over market since 1984. In 2015, he started recording audiobooks. Today, he has 28 books under his belt.

Unlike many of his colleagues, Flávio doesn't usually read the books before entering the studio. He says that his decision is not only due to a lack of time – there are works with up to a thousand pages, in addition to the books in series – but has to do with the desire not to spoil the surprise. "I know there are these recommendations to read before, but I think there's an enchantment when you come into contact with the book for the first time and that's what I try to convey to the reader.

It's been a wonderful experience to be a part of it. Book is something fantastic. We always learn. The great thing is to make this profession not only a livelihood, but a pleasure for us and, especially, for those who are listening."

9.4   Christian niche.

Since 1965 in the publishing market, Mundo TCriso decided to embark on audiobooks about a year ago.

There are already 20 titles that address religious issues, spirituality and even classic works in the public domain. "We realized that we couldn't just be a publisher of paper books. We had to be a content provider also in the digital world, with e-books, and in audio," says Renato Fleischer, director of Mundo Christian.

Fleischer predicts "a long future" for audiobooks, for their practicality. "More than reaching an audience with some visual impairment, it has conquered all kinds of people. Who's in traffic, who's not having much time to read, someone who's traveling.

A lot of people are already preferring the audiobook." The publisher's main narrator is Eduardo Costa Mendonça, better known as Duda Baguera. He has been working with voice for almost 30 years and began to have experience with audiobooks when he lived in the United States, at a time when the trend had not arrived in Brazil.

"The voice is a giant universe and each of the areas – dubbing, voice-over, narration – has its specificities," he points out. "In the case of the audiobook, you need to be the voice in the reader's head, but at the same time, not show up." Given the lack of courses in the area, Duda says that this is a trade that is learned in practice. "The more you do, the more you specialize," points out the narrator, who sees in the audiobook another benefit in addition to expanding the market for voice professionals. "In a country like ours, which is not so interested in reading, listening to the book can be a way to train readers."

9.5   Platforms.

Register on the platforms and start your career as an audio book narrator

Audiobook Creation Exchange is the publishing platform from Audible, an Amazon company, connecting the book-reading public's favorite stories to the actors who bring them to life. ACX was founded on the idea that every book and every voice deserves to be heard

With UBX - Ubook Exchange - narrators, actors and all voice professionals have a complete channel to secure new work. Thus, in addition to increasing their income, the narrator will also have their work made available on the largest audiobook platform in Latin America, to more than 1 million listeners worldwide.

Another way to find work is to sign up for freelance hiring sites like Workana and Upwork.

9.6 How Much Does a Book Narrator Make?

The professional chooses the amount they want to receive per hour produced or for the project as a whole, or even if they want to be paid for royalties from the sale of the audiobook.

You can receive a fixed amount for the narration or production work of an audio book (a payment for production), or you can agree to split the royalties with the rights holder and earn half of the royalties from each sale of the audio book.

But how much does the book narrator make at UBX?

The pay for this type of narration is often variable, depending on a number of factors. One of the main ones, without a doubt, is the length of the book, but it can also vary according to the language and the complexity of the work as a whole.

In general, it is a highly profitable branch with great possibilities of remuneration if the worker is committed and does his job well.

With this, you can look for specialized platforms and start doing the narration today. There are high chances that you will be well compensated for it in the long and medium term.

How do you get paid?

There are 3 ways to get paid for work as a narrator:

- Per finished hour (a flat-rate payment for the entire book).
- Royalty sharing (you split the royalties 50/50 with the author or "rights holder").
- Royalty share plus (a combination of royalty share and PFH).

9.7 How can you get started?

Here's what you need to do to get started:

- Gather the equipment.
- Create a free narrator profile on ACX.
- Set up a quiet space in your home for recording (cabinets work great).

- Create 1-3 audio samples to upload to your ACX profile.
- You can create audio samples using Audacity (which is free) or the professional recording software of your choice. Samples make your profile more complete and professional, so I recommend adding one or two to your profile before you start listening.
- Start auditioning for books available on ACX and keep doing so until you get your first offer.

9.8 How to choose the ideal studio for production?

Each production company has a style of recording and editing, ask more about the production company if they have had experience recording any audiobooks.

This question may seem simple, but it will make all the difference. Recording a spot or a 3-minute song is very different from recording a 10-hour audiobook. That's more than 60x more work when making an audiobook than a song.

Studio expertise is essential to ensure that the production is in line with the production's preparations.

The next question you need to ask is whether the studio is well insulated. Always doubt the acoustics, test, ask, feel the reverberation of the studio. The recording location is essential.

Clean pickup is essential for the quality of your audiobook. Any "external noise" cannot appear in the recording. The poor quality, the studio's pickup, and some other factors mentioned earlier will influence the final result of the audiobook.

For your audiobook project, it is necessary to pay attention to some details such as the quality of the studio, professionals and knowledge of the production company, as this will influence the final result of your audiobook.

10 WAY 8 - MAKE MONEY WITH AN ONLINE STORE.

An online store is, basically, an environment for commercial transactions on the Internet platform. But, let's face it, they are much more than that.

- It is a set of functionalities targeted at online commerce.
- It can be used on various platforms, such as notebook, desktop, mobile and tablets. There are no limits to its portability.

10.1 How to work with online stores.

A physical store has its own limits. It depends on infrastructure, location, environment, and publicity to be seen. The online store goes beyond these limits and offers its products on the web every day, 24 hours a day.

Since their emergence in the mid-1990s, virtual stores have caused a radical change in the retail trade.

By eliminating the physical presence of the buyer, seller and merchandise at the time of the transaction, the operation becomes faster and with several costs reduced.

This type of website depends on the qualities of your hosting service provider and should provide customers with a variety of payment options. Bank slips, paypal and credit cards are the most used means in this type of commerce.

If you have an online store or are planning to create one, stay tuned to our tips on customer service and learn how to make your customers more and more satisfied!

To open a Virtual Store it is not necessary to have an open company. The CPF is enough to open your store and start selling!

However, it should be noted that, regardless of the size of the company, it is important that you formalize the company and make the due accountability with the Federal Revenue Service.

Only then will it be possible to issue invoices and demonstrate your seriousness to your customers.

10.2 What does the customer expect from the online store's customer service?

When talking to an e-commerce, customers present some expectations that are normal in any segment and that can be observed through some basic points:

- The customer expects the person in charge of customer service to be committed to helping them with what they need;

- The customer expects the person in charge of the service to offer suggestions for proposals and improvements;
- The customer expects the person in charge of the service not to put their own interests over their own; and
- The customer expects the person in charge of the service to serve them with availability whenever necessary.

This may all seem simple at first glance, but research shows that most companies fail to satisfy at least 60% of their customers.

One of the main reasons for this is that those responsible for customer service do not have the required skills to perform their duties.

10.3   Types of online stores.

Types of online stores:

- Own store - exclusive sales space, customized by an agency or digital team.
- Store in a virtual mall - a store contracted with a sales site that aggregates other stores.
- Ready-made store - store created by the entrepreneur from ready-made templates.

The ready-made store is the most practical and accessible way to market your products on the internet.

In addition to easy creation and administration, many tools are free and the designs available are attractive.

10.4   Differential.

Sales systems can be purchased from third parties or developed in-house, but it is essential that they provide agile and efficient responses to users 365 days a year, 24 hours a day.

One way to avoid security problems is the certification of the website, in addition to other security measures already accessible to the entrepreneur on the internet.

It's important to keep in mind that the company-customer relationship starts before the sale and continues after the sale with loyalty that will bring the customer back for a next purchase.

Be sure to highlight the links to support in case of questions, returns, and exchanges. And be on the lookout for complaints. They provide important indications of how your store should improve.

Manage your inventory well. A very embarrassing situation is for you to sell a product that is out of stock. To avoid this situation, which testifies a lot against your online store, it is advisable that you constantly monitor the stock and change the status of unavailable products so that they are not purchased incorrectly by the customer.

It is also important to identify the products that sell the most and the sales behavior to have an efficient replenishment of inventory. The higher your conversion rate, the larger your inventory should be.

You should try to have as wide a variety of flags as possible, Paypal, boleto bancário and other forms that come up. If you don't offer some payment method that is preferred by the customer, they will give up on the purchase.

All they have to do is change sites to find another store that has the same product and accepts the payment method you don't have.

Keep an eye out for cases where someone didn't check out with the product in their cart. In many cases, the problem was the payment method. It is recommended to have at least three options of flags, boleto and debit. And be careful when choosing companies so as not to have difficulty with the approval of amounts or installments.

Figure 36 – Customer service makes all the difference.

Customer service should be cordial and very attentive. Whether by email, phone or chat, always start the dialogue with words like "hello" or "good afternoon" and end with "thank you" or "I am available".

Even if the customer asks questions that are already in the e-commerce description, take the time to answer them willingly. This is one of the characteristics that makes the consumer feel confident to buy from your company.

One of the most important points of customer service is after-sales, which applies to two different situations. The first is when the customer needs to exchange a product due to defect or dissatisfaction. In this case, your service should be similar to that of a sale, without treating it differently because it is an exchange.

The other case is when the purchase process was successful and your e-commerce wants to maintain the link with the consumer to build their loyalty. This relationship must be established in a genuine way, without excessive messages, which drive customers away more than they bring them closer.

When we talk about attending, we are talking about serving. To offer good customer service, the online store needs people who are happy to serve and who have the motivation to solve problems. In short, the doubts presented must be transformed into solutions.

For the customer, there is nothing more frustrating than buying a product that has problems and is not supported by a physical location by the brand. Customer service must be cordial and responsive enough to welcome the consumer and present a coherent way to solve any problem.

Good customer service should be marked by two words: friendliness and empathy. Both are linked to the concepts of involvement between people and are essential for perfect service.

While friendliness attracts and motivates the customer, empathy makes the attendant put himself in the consumer's shoes, seeking to get to know them better and serve them according to what they need and expect from the brand.

The professional who assists a client must express himself in a safe, clear, objective and transparent way. The information must be passed correctly and accurately, without making statements about which the agent is unsure.

Remember that deceiving the customer will make them never return to your store. On top of that, you still run the risk of him complaining on social media and rightly spreading the negative experience with the social circle.

10.5   Advantages and disadvantages.

Advantages.

- The internet has no geographical borders, meaning you can win customers from anywhere on the planet.
- In-stock products for e-commerce sites do not need to be displayed and can be stored compactly in a distribution center.
- An online store never closes.
- The internet is a medium that offers several tools for the relationship with the public, presentation of the business and improvement of the company's management.

Disadvantages.

1. No option to try the product

This is especially true for goods such as clothing and footwear.

In physical stores, we can try them at will, as well as being able to touch the piece, check its material, the quality... In virtual stores, on the other hand, the consumer has to be content with the images and description of the product.

Often, clothes and other items end up leaving something to be desired, due to quality, color difference, etc. After all, photos can be very deceiving! Therefore, it is essential to make an accurate description of your goods.

2. Insecurity on the part of customers

Although we live in the online age, many people are still "old-fashioned" in not buying from online stores. In some cases it may be due to lack of knowledge, but much of it is due to insecurity. Many consumers are afraid to buy from an unknown store for fear of not receiving the product or even of informing their personal and bank details.

3. Product delays and damage

At least once you will suffer from the delay of your products, and it will not be your fault, but the carriers. This delay is common, and unfortunately some more fragile goods are subject to being damaged during transport, causing the consumer to be disappointed when receiving the order.

To prevent this from happening, it is essential to pack your goods well, wrapping them in cardboard or any other resistant material, which makes the product box firm, and that the product does not become "loose" and swaying inside the package.

In any case, even with these disadvantages, it is totally possible to convert these situations, preventing yourself to avoid major problems and complaints. These factors will be judicious for the success or not of your business

Below, we will explain how these and other strategies work for you to get your hands dirty and create your online business. Check!

10.6   Choice of product mix.

The first step is to know what you're going to sell. The choice of these products is indicated from your initial investment. If you want to have a shoe e-commerce, but you can't start with more elaborate shoes, how about selling sneakers? Thus, you expand your business according to your growth.

Ideally, the mix of products or services chosen should be something you know, facilitating the process of choices, such as prices, ideal stock, advertising and promotion material.

10.7   Steps to create your online store.

10.7.1 Definition of the name of the online store.

Once you know what you're going to sell, choose a name that's consistent with the industry. For example, if your store sells sneakers for women who wear shoes between 34 and 35, the name of the business could be "Princess Foot."

Once the name is defined, create a logo identifying the predominant colors. At Bertholdo, for example, a shade of purple was used that accompanies all the materials that represent the brand.

The name of the online store should also be appropriate to the audience, being attractive and easy to remember. A common mistake is to adopt terms that are not well understood, such as English words, when the audience is made up of simpler people.

10.7.2 Competitor analysis.

The next step can be done in conjunction with the first and second, since the information collected in it can influence both decisions. It consists of understanding the competition, that is, which other companies already sell the selected mix of products online.

To do this, do online searches about the items and the region in which you want to sell and understand the sales strategy of each competitor to identify opportunities and threats to your business. For example, if they all offer free shipping, it is very recommended that your online store also has this benefit to attract consumers. Thus, this cost has to be considered in your sales strategy.

10.7.3 Selection of the e-commerce platform

Now is the time to select the platform for the development of your store. There are many options available and the choice should be made considering the cost-effectiveness, the features offered, the support and the strategy of your venture.

10.7.4 Customization of the online store

With the platform already chosen, set up your store with the tones of the visual identity and align the modules that will be necessary for the operation of your e-commerce — such as Correios, boleto, credit and debit cards.

At this point, you need to optimize your store according to your needs. The important thing is to monitor the usability of your website with customers, so it will never be outdated. Therefore, try to study more about the reasons for you to keep your online store always up to date.

10.7.5 Inclusion of product images and descriptions

Once you've customized your online store's system and visual identity, it's time to include images, descriptions, and information about your products. Ideally, the photos should have a high resolution and be able to show the attributes of each item.

In addition, it is recommended that the descriptions follow good SEO practices (Search Engine Optimization, in Portuguese), which is nothing more than adopting keywords used by customers in their searches, being direct, informative, creative and objective.

To better understand, in the example of size 34 or 35 sneakers, a good title for one of the items would be "Moleca Sneakers Size 34" and its description "Buy Moleca Sneakers Size 34 in Pé de Princesa. Free shipping from R$ 150. We deliver all over Brazil."

10.7.6 Security for the online store

It is important to note that the security of your online store is one of the main factors for customer loyalty. Therefore, keep in mind that your e-commerce must be constantly updated. One tip is to hire a company specialized in the area, so you won't take risks and will also avoid inconvenience.

Still talking about security, one of the features to be highlighted is the encrypted environment, which allows people from all over the world to buy from your online store without the risk of data leakage. This protection is only possible through the SSL certificate – Security Socket Layer.

10.7.6.1 Definition of the marketing plan

One of the main mistakes of a new entrepreneur is not having a set budget for the marketing team. Ideally, a monthly amount should be set aside to invest in communication and dissemination actions for your e-commerce.

This amount may be small, but it is indispensable. For its optimization, it is recommended to have a clear investment plan, with a calendar of actions for the period (month, quarter, etc.). Positive examples of activities include buying online ads and promoting social media posts.

It is part of the marketing activities to think about the product descriptions and the budget investment plan, as well as to create and manage social networks and define customer relationship strategies, ensuring their satisfaction and loyalty.

So let's start by determining the cost of the e-commerce platform, the heart of the entire business. This is a cost that will depend a lot on the size of the business you intend to set up and the resources you will need.

Figure 37 – Add to cart.

You will actually have three options of platforms to set up your online store:

- Plataformas open source.
- Leased platforms – SaaS.
- Exclusive platforms.

In open source e-commerce platforms, open-source systems that you can download, install and configure, there are numerous options available on the market.

Although it sounds simple, you actually need to have a very good knowledge of programming to be able to properly install more sophisticated systems like Magento. So, don't be fooled, you will need to hire a programmer or specialized company.

So that you can get an idea of how much it costs to set up an online store using the Magento Commerce solution, a good professional or specialized company charges around R$ 10,000 to install and configure the system.

On the other hand, in the category of rented virtual stores, the dispersion of prices is very large. There are dozens of suppliers with the most diverse proposals, and therefore it is necessary to analyze each one in detail so as not to make a mistake in the choice. There are several factors to take into consideration.

For those who want to know how much it costs to set up a virtual store with a rented e-commerce platform, we can tell you that the initial starts at around R$ 30.00 and can reach up to more than R$ 8,000 in the most sophisticated models.

Here's an important tip. You don't choose an e-commerce platform for its price, but for the features and other technical aspects it offers. The ideal is to ask for a quote for an e-commerce platform from several suppliers and analyze their proposals well.

Lastly, you would have the option of an exclusive platform. In this case, there is no way to say what the price level is, since the budget depends on numerous factors. What we can say is that the investment is very high and therefore not advisable for those who are just starting out.

10.8   Once the store is set up, it's time to advertise the business.

With the online store and marketing strategy ready, it's time to launch and start promoting it to attract consumers. Ideally, you should use performance indicators to measure the efficiency of each channel and each strategy used.

The use of metrics allows the manager to evaluate best practices and better direct the company's budget. Thus, the most sought-after products can gain prominence in the virtual store and undergo price modifications to increase satisfaction and sales results.

10.8.1 The big cost of an online store is in the promotion of the business.

As Jerry Young, one of the founders of Yahoo, used to say, a website without advertising is like a billboard in the basement of the house, no one sees it.

In the specific case of e-commerce, we have some areas that cannot be left out in an online marketing strategy:

- SEO – Optimization of websites for search engines.
- Sponsored Links – Paid ads on Google and other channels.
- E-mail marketing.
- Social media.

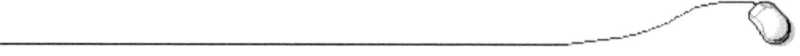

10.8.2 The cost of promoting the online store.

Setting up an e-commerce without worrying about the promotion of the virtual store is the famous shot in the foot. If in the physical store everyone is worried about advertising, why act differently when it comes to creating a virtual store. They need a lot of outreach, whether it's through SEO or SEM strategies.

If you can't get listed in search engines in prominent positions, it greatly compromises the success of the business.

Digital marketing plays a key role in the business plan of any e-commerce project nowadays. To overlook this cost variable of an online store is not to take your own project seriously.

Within any planning, this budget must be determined very carefully, because in the first moments of the store the use of digital marketing is quite intensive. E-commerce training is an investment.

10.8.3 Customer journey mapping.

Mapping the customer journey is the process of identifying the journey they take from the first contact with your online store to the moment they make a purchase. This allows you to understand, for example, the reasons that lead the user to abandon the cart or not close a deal.

The mapping involves everyone who has direct contact with the consumer, so that you can have a complete view of what they expect from the company and what, in fact, they receive.

10.8.4 Ad spend.

Ads are a paid media strategy that can be very useful for those who are starting an online store. In Google Ads, Google's ad platform, you can create them for an audience segmented according to the most useful keywords to find your brand in search results.

That way, whenever the user searches for certain terms, Google will show your ads at the top of the search results, ensuring more and more traffic to your online store. Best of all, you only pay for each click.

10.8.5 Investment in mobile.

Mobile is no longer just a trend in e-commerce to become a fundamental strategy to attract customers. A recent survey shows that 85% of Brazilians with a smartphone shop online. With the increase in the public that makes purchases on the internet, this number tends to grow in the coming years.

Having mobile operations, adapted to different mobile devices, ensures that consumers will have good shopping experiences regardless of the device they use. When your website isn't responsive, your pages often take a long time on mobile devices, which drives potential customers away.

10.9   Clarity in the privacy policy.

The privacy policy should be a priority for those who want to set up an online store or for those who are in the process of perfecting one that is already active. This is a document that should explain how the company collects, stores, protects, manipulates, and shares its user's data.

In addition to ensuring more credibility and more transparency in the relationship with the public, the document allows the virtual store to meet legal obligations. The General Data Protection Law (LGPD) and the Brazilian Civil Rights Framework for the Internet are, for example, two standards that attest to the need to have a clear privacy policy.

11 WAY 9 – MAKE MONEY ON BUYING AND SELLING SITES.

One of the best ideas to make money fast is to sell things online. For example, you can sell clothing, furniture, and bags from your own home, or buy and resell higher-value items such as laptops, TVs, or phones.

You can buy these products online from sites like AliExpress or from local thrift stores and thrift stores – a great way to make money quickly and make extra money.

Some of the most searched buying and selling sites are OLX, Mercado Libre, Enjoei, and eBay. These sites charge a fairly small fee on top of your profit.

To sell on sites like this, you need to choose a product that is not so easily found in any store, and that you can buy it for a competitive price to be able to add to your profit margin and still remain competitive compared to the physical store.

Many people use this way of making money online and make a lot of money every day.

Tips for selling a lot:

- Take great quality photos, which allow a complete view of the product;
- Have a well-crafted description, to convince the customer to buy your merchandise;
- Offer warranty;
- Have different payment options;
- Inform how the product will be delivered;
- Use good boxes and packaging;
- It is important to find good suppliers, who have regularity in stock and delivery, have quality products and with differentiated prices for wholesale. This way you will be able to make a good profit on the sale.

PARA QUEM COMPRA

 Pesquise preços: para saber se vale a pena levar o produto, cheque a faixa de preço da mesma peça na coleção atual. Com essa noção, você decide se a compra é uma boa opção

 É necessário ter muita cautela para não comprar produtos não originais. Pergunte ao vendedor se ele oferece garantia e nota fiscal

 Como você desconhece a origem dos produtos, pode levar um susto ao descobrir, principalmente no caso de eletrônicos, que são falsos ou até roubados

 Pense na forma de pagamento antes de efetuar a compra

 Invista naquilo que realmente precisa: sair comprando só porque achou peças mais baratas do que o habitual acaba fazendo com que gaste ainda mais

 No caso de eletrônicos, redobre sua atenção: observe um botão com mau contato, uma tela trincada ou uma bateria que já não dura tanto ou verifique se o aparelho está lento, para de funcionar ou esquenta muito

 Salve e imprima todo o processo de compra. Assim, caso a aquisição não chegue até você, terá todas as provas de que efetuou o pagamento

 Conexão segura: veja se a página têm conexão de segurança. Para fazer isso, basta verificar se o site começa com **https://**

PARA QUEM VENDE

 Para precificar, observe quando pagou pelo produto novo e considere o modelo, a idade e a marca

 Não minta ou esconda se houver defeitos na peça

 Seja direto e sincero na descrição do produto

 Para negociar, você pode fixar o preço com uma margem que seja interessante

 Faça uma pesquisa de mercado com similares novos e usados

 Cuide da exposição do produto. Uma boa fotografia e uma iluminação adequada valorizam os produtos

 Para sua segurança, se tiver que encontrar o comprador, marque num local bastante movimentado, como um shopping

 Procure sites para fazer a cotação online

Figure 38 – Success tips for those who buy and those who sell.

All these details must be developed with full attention, as they are essential to sell more and gain loyal customers

But be careful!

Don't quit your job to do this unless you know you're going to succeed and already have regular buyers.

It's best to do your research to make sure you're getting a great deal and aren't getting scammed. If you're meeting people face-to-face, make sure they are trustworthy.

11.1 To be a good Internet marketer, pay attention to these tips.

11.1.1 Decide what you want to buy and sell.

You can sell a variety of things, but it's best to specialize in one market.

You can buy and sell almost anything. You can buy and sell material things, such as oranges and umbrellas, or non-material things, such as a service or a business interest.

Remember a few principles. The rarer something is, the more people will pay for it if they want or need it. This is called supply and demand. In this way, a natural diamond costs more than an artificial one, because natural diamonds are much rarer.

The more work or expertise that goes into a product or service, the more it will cost. Something that takes a long time to do, or something that can only be offered with several degrees of expertise or a long workout, will cost a lot more than something that can be done by anyone.

11.1.2 Research the market.

You absolutely need to know the average price of your product when selling it or buying it from someone who knows its value.

The markets where you can do the research can be retail stores, wholesale, internet, or other evaluators. If you can, see how the value of the product is in the sales and purchases of open marketplaces, such as Ebay or Mercado Libre.

The market value of your product or service will fluctuate from time to time depending on a number of circumstances. While the price of milk has changed little in the last ten years, the prices of gold and crude oil have changed considerably.

11.1.3 Find a supplier to source your goods.

Make sure that such a supplier is reliable and that they will sell the products to you for a lower price than you will get when reselling.

These suppliers will usually sell wholesale. Someone who sells wholesale is usually an intermediary who buys the items and sells them to someone who works in retail (changing little or no value), and who subsequently sells them to a customer.

If you can buy products directly from the manufacturer, you cut out the middleman and can typically make more money from your product. Whenever possible, try to buy your product directly from the manufacturer, as this way you don't have to pay the middleman's part.

11.1.4 Buy cheap, sell for a better price.

Pay attention to the market so you know exactly when to sell. You must find a market that is sustainable, and that you can count on.

As a rule of thumb, you want to buy low and sell high. This means buying your product at the lowest possible price and selling it at the highest possible price. This will give you the most profit.

There are a few caveats to this rule. Generally, when you buy a product for a cheaper price, the quality of the product is not that good. So, for example, you can buy an umbrella for $10 and sell it to someone for $30 and that will mean you bought low and sold high.

But, the quality of your umbrella may not be good. You could, however, buy a high-quality umbrella for $30 and sell it to someone else for $100. You'll probably make fewer individual sales this way, but the total profit from your sales may be higher.

11.2   Buying and selling sites on the Internet.

Try to sell your products on multiple platforms and marketplaces instead of just one. The more places your products are, the more likely people are to find them.

There are hundreds of online selling sites, all with their own niches and commission rates. Some examples are:

1. Free market.

MercadoLibre allows you to sell just about anything, and the best part: without having to pay for the ad. For used products, you will always be able to advertise and sell for free, without paying any fees.

In addition, the first announcements of new products on the platform are also free. Advertisers can create "infinite" ads, with no time limit. The site has apps that run on Android and iOS.

2. I got seasick.

Enjoei is a great way to sell your products, because in addition to having a very nice layout, the tool often offers a series of discounts to encourage the flow of purchases and sales.

Not only does this make you more likely to buy something at a good discount, but it also attracts buyers. Despite not charging for the ad, the site keeps 20% of the sales.

3. OLX.

OLX is home to the former Bom Negócios website. Now, with the two together, the services have created an even better tool. The site also does not charge anything for the advertisement of a product, and automatically advertises for several states in Brazil, which increases the chances of sales.

Unlike MercadoLibre, it works as a classifieds and does not mediate financial transactions.

4. Uzlet.

Uzlet is restricted to smartphones only. The proposal is to stop keeping old cell phones in the drawer at home and make money with them. To start selling, simply register on the site and select what you want to sell. Once sold, simply send it to the new owner by post office.

5. It takes off.

The name of the site says it all. No more clinging to that outfit that no longer fits or that piece of furniture that doesn't match the sofa. The tool offers several categories, such as men, women, children, news, and promotions.

However, unlike some sites, such as Enjoei, which already pays the user's shipping, in Desapego the shipping is the seller's responsibility. He is the one who must bear the shipping costs and request a refund after the product has been delivered to its final destination.

6. I caught Goat.

The platform arose from the partnership between sisters Gabriela and Daniela Carvalho, who started the online sales site for used parts. Unlike the others, Peguei Bode is best known for having designer brands such as Hermés, Chanel, Prada, Gucci and Balenciaga.

7. How cheap.

Que Barato offers customers a secure way to post ads for free and without commission. In it, you will find offers on different products such as cars, motorcycles, trucks – used and new – as well as opportunities for houses and

apartments in your region. The sheer diversity is a very attractive part of the site, but not everyone likes it. The service has a lot of ads, which makes it difficult to search for new things, but nothing that compromises.

12 FORM 10 - CONTENT CREATOR FOR THE WEB.

The Content Creator is the professional who produces content on the internet, whether in text, video, image or audio format. Think of that pastry chef who creates videos teaching delicious recipes on Facebook or the blogger who travels the world and posts tips on the best destinations on her blog. And yet, do you follow that financial expert who gives investment tips on his Youtube channel?

Figure 39- The creator cloud.

That's that! In case you don't know, they are examples of content creators, who teach or entertain their audience on the internet, sharing what they know how to do best: entertain or teach with their knowledge and talents!

It is necessary for you to realize that in order to stand out as a web content creator, it is necessary to:

- Dominate social media.
- Write quality content that is targeted to the brand's audience.
- Develop persuasive writing.
- Use SEO techniques.
- Know a lot about Inbound Marketing.
- Understand what customers want to see on the brand page.
- Have a portfolio always available to show your skills as a content producer and get more opportunities.

But note that it takes a lot of work, patience and dedication to succeed, because only then will the results come. However, this alone is not enough, you must focus on something that brings real and sustainable gains to you, as that is the goal.

But why is this profession on the rise nowadays? In this post, we'll tell you the reasons why content creators have become the darlings of brands to promote their products, and how you can take advantage of this profession.

12.1 Understand the origin of the profession.

The good root user of the internet, who has been working with digital marketing for some time, must remember Flogão or Fotolog. In these blogs, we saw the first traces of what we now understand as digital influencers.

Ordinary people posted photos and texts about their days. Some drew more attention than others and ended up attracting followers from different parts of the country — which really was a great feat in the days of dial-up internet.

After that, Orkut became a fever and the creators of the most popular communities were the famous ones on the internet. Some bloggers have also started to stand out since then, such as Taci Alcolea and Mari Moon. Then came YouTube and Twitter; and then Face-book and Instagram.

It's not new that brands team up with people of relevance online to bring their products to more people. However, the professionalization of this type of service has certainly reached unprecedented levels.

12.2 The current scenario - co-creation.

Precisely because of this professionalization, the demands of both parties — brands and content creators — have grown a lot.

On the one hand, people with a legion of followers saw a great opportunity to generate income from these numbers; Brands, in turn, began to charge more neat deliveries to justify the high investment.

Figure 40 - Co-creation allows for collaborative work.

Thus, the idea of influencing simply for the sake of influencing began to make less and less sense. What we see instead is the idea of co-creation. The union of brands and content creators must be something really organic and that makes sense for the influencer's audience.

The vast majority of these people gain notoriety and relevance because of the creation of spontaneous content. Thus, the public soon notices cases in which the person discloses something that they probably do not consume, which can be harmful to both the brand and the content creator.

Now it's time to choose what type of Content Creator you'll be:

1. Influencer.

Generally speaking, a digital influencer is someone who has an active profile on at least one social network. To be considered as such, you must, at the very least, have a relevant number of followers and a large volume of publications and interactions.

We can also stick to the meaning of the word. In this way, an influencer is also that person who makes — or has the potential to make — a difference in a purchase decision or in the formation of an opinion, for example.

2. Micro influencer.

As the name says, the micro influencer plays the same role as the influencer, but on a smaller spectrum. The most common is that this influencer has a local relevance, still restricted to a single city or state.

There is no consensus on the number of followers and this parameter depends on the interests of the brand. However, we can consider that those who have up to 50 thousand followers belong to this category. These influencers can be great allies of regional brands, especially due to their proximity to the intended audience of these companies.

Thaynara OG, for example, started as a micro influencer in São Luiz, until she burst onto Snapchat and became a sensation across the country.

3. Content creator.

Be careful, because here the definitions get more complex. To be considered a content creator, the influencer needs to offer something to their followers. Yes, it's possible to influence without offering content — and we have some examples below.

The content creator is the one who uses their social networks (or even other platforms) to add some value to what they offer to their followers, even in cases where there is no brand promoting this.

Here we are talking, for example, about bloggers who always publish travel tips, instagramers who bring tips on looks and youtubers who talk about the most varied subjects.

4. Celebrity.

Celebrities are perhaps the prime examples of influencers who don't produce content. Bruna Marquezine, for example, already has more than 36 million followers, makes several paid partnerships with brands on her Instagram, but we can't say that she is a content creator.

Still not convinced? Fernanda Souza and Giovanna Ewbank can offer us a good counterpoint. The two are actresses and presenters and have certainly gained their many followers because of their work on the small screen. However, they also have YouTube channels, they dedicate time, energy, and money to planning and producing this content.

5. Authority.

In general, authorities are those influencers who have gained relevance on social networks because of some work they were already doing outside of it. They can also be content creators or not. Generally, the topics covered are more segmented, as well as their audiences.

The Dibradoras, for example, were already sports journalists when they came together to create profiles to talk about women in sports. Karen Jonz is a four-time world champion in skateboarding, so there is no one better than her to talk about this sport on a YouTube channel. In this case, they are a reference in a subject in which they also create content.

Paola Carosella, on the other hand, is an influencer and top reference in cooking, organic food and the like. However, so far, she is not exactly a content creator — but she already has a very active participation in Twitter and there are indications that she should start a project on YouTube.

6. Journalist.

Inevitably, journalists are opinion makers. With the popularization of social networks, they also become digital influencers. What examples? Evaristo Costa and Dony De Nuccio.

But then they're influencer journalists and not content creators, right? That's right! But there are also those who create content, such as Cris Bartis and Juliana Wallauer, anchors of the Mamilos podcast, who are there to prove it.

7. Blogger.

Blogging has long ceased to be just a digital diary and has become a great business opportunity. For this reason, it's possible that you work as a content creator with a focus on being a blogger. In this case, it is necessary that, first of all, you establish a theme for your blog and the ideal is that you have an affinity with it.

After all, if you are passionate about your field and have an affinity for it, your content will be attractive. In this way, you will be able to attract traffic to your blog, being able to earn money through partnerships with companies, which is done through banners and advertising.

In addition, being a blogger makes it possible for you to sign up for Google Adsense, where you bill for displaying ads within your page.

8. Video producer for YouTube.

Making money on the internet as a content creator can be done easily by producing videos for Youtube.

Well, it is no wonder that today there are millionaire creators, such as Whindersson Nunes and Felipe Neto, for example.

Obviously, it takes years to get to such a level, but everything had a beginning, the first step, and that's exactly what you should do: start without fear.

So, try to identify a niche within Youtube that you identify with and start producing the videos, do it quite often and dedicatedly.

In this way, the time will come when the platform itself will deliver its content to people.

With this, you earn money through brands that will seek you out for partnerships. After all, you have the channel, the audience and so they will naturally want you to make the famous "advertli".

In addition to this path, Youtube itself has its reward mechanism, which is done through ad views.

Therefore, there will be no shortage of ways to make money with this platform for you who want to create video content.

9. Instagram digital influencer.

In addition to the paths mentioned above, which are promising, you can still earn money creating content for Instagram, thus being a digital influencer on this social network.

Figure 41 – Digital influencer.

In case you didn't know, a digital influencer is a person who can influence thousands of people on social media.

To do this, it has a high engagement, which is done through:

- Comments;
- Tanned;
- Shares.

Thus, it becomes recognized, drawing the attention of brands, which close partnerships so that they create exclusive content of offers and promotions.

10. Podcast producer.

Podcasts are similar to radio shows, but they are disseminated on the internet, which means that they have a much greater reach.

Today there are people who produce audio content and make a lot of money from it.

After all, audiences like to listen, especially when topics that are of interest to them are addressed. So, you just need to focus on producing a podcast within an area that you know and have an affinity for. Some of the most consumed forms of podcasts are debates and interviews. In addition to humorous content, which is always welcome.

This is a content format that requires a little more work, since it encompasses soundtrack editing, cuts, among others. However, there are already free tools that do this job and can help automate your podcasts.

In addition, once the audio content is ready, you just have to insert it within a platform, such as Spotify, and disseminate it so that people start listening to it.

And how do you make money from podcasts?

Through advertising, as companies close recurring partnerships with this type of content creator, especially when they have an engaged audience.

12.3 What are the advantages of hiring a Content Creator?

Now that you know more about the professionalization of a content creator, keep in mind that you shouldn't enter into this type of partnership just because all brands are investing in it.

In fact, there are different advantages that both influencers and creators can bring to a brand, whether it is large, medium or small.

Even digital entrepreneurs can benefit from this type of negotiation in promoting their digital products. Here's how!

12.4 Reach.

We already know that Creators have a lot to offer brands, especially when we consider the idea of co-creation. However, not so long ago, the main attraction of internet celebrities was the legion of fans they dragged.

That is, the greater the number of followers, the greater the need to invest in that person. Today, however, we already understand that engagement also plays a key role in conversion, although creator reach cannot be entirely discarded.

These people speak to many people and in a personal, unique, captivating and original tone; something that many brands try, but few actually manage to do.

Increasingly, working with a Content Creator is understood as a partnership. The parties involved should work together to co-create something that is relevant to both the brand's audience and the content creator's audience.

Piggybacking on the idea of a good relationship between Creator and fan base, this same thought should apply between brands and content creators. The idea is that this type of partnership is always beneficial to both sides.

In other words, while the Creator generates income, the brand increases its reach and improves the chances of conversion. In this way, investing in a long-term relationship can have great benefits.

12.5   New consumption rules.

Digital transformation has changed the way we relate to each other and has also brought new rules of consumption.

In this context, since the days of the late Fotolog and Orkut, digital influencers have begun to gain popularity and attract the interest of brands that intend to reach new audiences through these partnerships.

With a large number of followers, this type of partnership brings several benefits to brands and also to creators, who can generate income from the content they already produced. In addition, the idea of co-creation also gains more strength and content creators become more demanded in terms of quality of delivery and result.

12.6   It's not all spotlights: there are laws!

We can say that Content Creation is a new profession, without any provision in the law so far. There are two bills aimed at regulating the profession of blogger and vlogger, PLs 4289/2016 and 8569/2017.

While a specific law is not approved, the rules for the provision of services that have legal provisions in the Civil Code, the Consumer Protection Code, the Copyright Law, the Civil Rights Framework for the Internet, CONAR rules and other applicable rules are used.

To reduce the risk of the judiciary recognizing an employment relationship, it is recommended that the contract for the provision of services between the

Influencer and the Contractor include clauses of autonomy and independence, but remembering that for the judiciary what really matters is the way the service is carried out in practice.

12.7 And how to get started?

Being successful is not easy and you need to follow a few steps to start your work as a Content Creator:

1. Define your niche well;
2. Create your buyer PERSONA, which represents your "ideal" consumer;
3. Choose the platforms or networks on which you will post your content;
4. Do trend and keyword research to guide your production;
5. Establish a fixed schedule of publications;
6. Acquire the necessary equipment (such as a good camera, in case you are going to record videos);
7. Produce, produce, produce!
8. Use marketing strategies to promote your content.

13 WAY 11 – MAKE MONEY AS SOCIAL MEDIA.

Social Media is nothing more than the professional responsible for managing social networks. Perhaps one of the main challenges – if not the biggest one – of Social Media is to convey to the public on the networks the essence of a product and its brand.

Being in the role of managing a company's profiles on social networks, the professional can develop several activities. Such as:

1. Promote products: think of creative ways to present products and services and their differentials.
2. Sell products: Facebook and Instagram have the option to create online stores and reach the public much more easily, making it a great source of revenue.
3. Promote interaction: regardless of the social network, promoting interaction with the target audience and generating engagement should be the main objective.

Figure 42 – The universe of Social Media work.

For a relevant performance, the professional who works as social media must understand the dynamics of social networks. Deeply understanding the behavior of the target audience and the company's culture makes the process much easier.

The communication used in social media cannot be disconnected from what the organization really is.

Social Media also needs to know the particularities of each network:

- Twitter has a limited number of characters;
- Facebook uses a system of algorithms to distribute content within the platform.

Understanding and analyzing the metrics of each social network is essential for a good performance in this profession, as well as mastering the use of the main tools for social media management.

13.1   What this professional is and what he does.

According to a survey by Hootsuite and We are Social, 62% of the Brazilian population is active on social networks.

YouTube leads the list of the most accessed social networks by Brazilians, concentrating 60% of accesses. Facebook, which appears first in other surveys, comes right after, in second position, with 59%.

WhatsApp is in third place with 56 percent, followed by Instagram in fourth with 40 percent.

Thinking about taking advantage of this new reality of the consumer market, companies understood that they need to be on social networks. Therefore, they have been investing in strategies to make their presence even more relevant there.

Whether it's to improve customer relationships or increase reach and sales, with digital marketing comes the social media profession.

13.2 What does social media mean?

Social media means social media. That is, digital communication channels through which interactions, collaboration, and content sharing take place. These are platforms that function as repositories of content that need human interaction to come to life.

Figure 43 – Social media.

For exactly the same reason, they have become powerful channels for companies to reach a more qualified audience and, thus, increase brand perception with authority and achieve success among customers.

With the advancement of the digital age, the meaning of social media has gained a new possibility: it has become a profession.

13.3 What does a social media professional do?

The social media professional is responsible for activating these channels for public persons, companies, or even personal projects. He is the one who plans and creates content to be shared on social networks and also publishes within these platforms, interacts with other users, analyzes results and makes everything happen.

You hear about the social media profession and think that to succeed in it, you just have to scroll through social media all day long. But as you can see, it goes far beyond being a heavy user. It requires the professional to always be up-to-date on social media news and market trends.

13.4 What is the academic background of this professional?

In general, the social media professional can be trained in both the field of social communication and administration. Most of them have academic backgrounds in Journalism, Letters, Marketing, Advertising or Public Relations. But that doesn't mean that that social media expert with a degree in Business Administration can't invest in their career.

To become a successful social media, the tip is very objective: study hard and dedicate yourself to knowing the main trends in digital marketing. Even if the profession seems like a dream, you must love social media. And not only that: you must know how to get people interested in the pages you manage.

13.5 The routine of a social media.

To increase the quality of social media work, it is essential to create a daily routine of activities. A way to facilitate the synchronization between professional functions and skills to the requirements and expectations of the client served.

Functions that are part of the routine of a successful social media:

1. Posting schedule.

Creating and maintaining an up-to-date posting schedule is the best way to meet timely customer needs. Thus, it is possible to plan the content to be shared and even anticipate certain actions.

2. Produce content.

Here we are talking about the production of institutional or promotional content for the client. A job that requires creativity and technical knowledge about design and available formats to engage users.

3. Distribute impactful content across networks.

With the content produced, it's time to distribute what social media has at hand. As each social network has a specificity, it is necessary to keep in mind that the contents cannot be the same.

If on Facebook, for example, the company will work on ads to increase its reach, on LinkedIn, it will attract and retain talent. While the first gives visibility and promotes engagement, the second is business.

As there are several social networks, a lot of content to be produced and more than one customer to be served, controlling the delivery of content requires attention and patience.

So that the task does not become exhausting, it can be made easier with the use of media managers. Some of them are: Buffer, Hootsuite, and TweetDeck. Platforms that help you concentrate content distribution in one place. They optimize the social media routine.

4. Do daily monitoring.

Monitoring work helps the social media professional measure, analyze, and compile information to identify opportunities and weaknesses. It is an important activity for the company to be able to carry out corrective actions.

To make it easier to check performance, I'll go back to the social media management programs. They make it possible for social media to analyze key social media metrics, as well as offer features such as replying to comments and private messages.

5. Prepare performance reports.

The production of performance reports for social networks is a result of monitoring work. Of course, the better the numbers raised by social media, the more satisfied the customer will be.

But it is essential not to "make up" this data. After all, just as they can reflect the success of the work done, they also help identify the need for improvement.

13.6 Tools and software used by social media.

Since everything happens in real time, sometimes it is humanly impossible to optimize activities and processes. But there are tools and software to make things easier.

Check out some of them below:

- Competitor Analysis: Alexa, Ubersuggest, and SEMrush
- Visual content creation: Canva, IM Free, and Unsplash
- Content curation: Flipboard, Pearltrees, and Storify
- Social media management: the aforementioned Buffer, Hootsuite and TweetDeck, as well as mLabs
- Metrics monitoring: Google Analytics, HubSpot and RD Station.

It is also important to remember that social networks themselves offer very useful tools for social media. Face-book Ads and Instagram for Business are examples.

To make the right choice, try to understand what features you need and what makes sense for your project. Some social media tools and software offer trial versions. It is usually a shortcut so that you can get to know its features and understand what best fits your needs.

If your performance is punctual and limited, it may not be worth investing in more complete tools. But if you deal with more than one account and a large number of followers, it makes perfect sense to set aside part of the budget for that.

13.7 How much does a social media professional make?

According to salary estimates published on the Vagas website, the average gross salary of a social media employee is R$ 2,152.00[14]. The salary of a social media analyst, on the other hand, is around R$ 3,969.00.

---

[14] Values as of October 2022.

But the remuneration depends on several factors: whether the professional works in an agency, is self-employed or outsourced, for example. So, it can be bigger, the more skilled and specialized the social media is.

13.8 What is the job market like?

The job market for the social media professional is constantly on the rise. This is because, in the information age, the number of users present on social networks is increasing.

But, just as it is a profession that is currently on the rise, it is also quite competitive. Therefore, the tip is to always be up to date and not settle.

Social media start-ups, for example, can more easily get jobs in startups and small businesses. On the other hand, the most advanced ones find opportunities even in companies with an exclusive internal sector for these demands.

The coolest thing about this profession is that it is not restricted only to the corporate market. Then, the professional in the area can work as a freelancer or even become an individual microentrepreneur (MEI).

13.9 Top ways to make money as a social media.

As there are still companies that do not have qualified professionals to work with social media, here are the opportunities:

1. Social media management.

The social media manager has the responsibility of creating strategies to reach the audience of interest and sell your products or services.

As such, you must monitor and stay on top of what happens on different channels at the same time.

2. Manage your own project.

Another opportunity to make money as a social media appears by offering your own services through social networks.

Are you a master of content, design, programming or are you a digital marketing consultant? Try using these channels to spread the word about what you do best. The results may be surprising.

3. Design for social media.

Not every company has a design professional at their disposal to create amazing art and meet their social media goals. But this type of work is essential for ads and publications to become more attractive to the audience and potential customers.

So, specializing in social media design is an interesting way to differentiate yourself from the competition. After all, not every social media knows how to build quality art.

If you're good at graphic design, you can even become a social media partner to take care of the visual part of the clients served.

13.10   But think about it!

Even though it is a relatively recent area of marketing, today, every company is interested in promoting products and services on social networks.

And the social media professional tends to be increasingly valued to meet business needs with the expertise that only he has.

Figure 44 – The world of social media work.

Acting as a Social Media requires a lot of study and frequent updating of your knowledge. Because it is still a fairly new area, but one that is beginning to gain recognition, a lot is happening all the time.

Social media is particularly vulnerable to problems interacting with technology. It should be noted:

1. Develop Upgrade Syndrome.
2. Develop relationship problems due to social media.
3. Suffering from infidelity on social media.
4. Suffer from privacy issues.
5. Reduce academic ability.
6. Being a victim of cybercrime and bullying.
7. Falling in love with fake identities.
8. Neglecting family and responsibilities.
9. Develop addiction to online friends.
10. Lose the power of Focus and Productivity.
11. Develop FOMO syndrome.
12. Addict to online games.
13. Develop psychological problems.
14. Spending too much time on social media.
15. Getting addicted to social media.

14 WAY 12 – MAKE MONEY AS AN SEO MANAGER.

Knowing how to rank websites and make them appear in the first results and pages of search engines is a very lucrative skill. The more people are interested in using search engines, the more people will be interested in learning more about SEO.

The professional specialized in SEO needs to have knowledge of the various search engines and needs to have as a basis that the analysis of keywords constitutes the basis to maximize the results of search engines.

It is necessary to know the digital marketing tools and know how to reach the right conclusions from the results of the keyword analysis.

Figure 45 - Be an SEO manager.

Another essential factor for SEO success is knowing how to use language, spelling, and grammar well in order to explain complex subjects in a simple, seductive, and exciting way.

Thus, this is the same as saying that the professional needs to know how to place himself as belonging to the target audience of the content to be written.

To be successful, posts, text, polls, and images must offer consumers true added value around their interests. Empathy must be present to some degree.

SEO is the acronym for "Search Engine Optimization".

Being an SEO manager implies being a professional who uses various strategies in order to enhance and improve the positioning of a website in the organic results of search engines.
There are two categories of SEO methods:

1. White Hat. They use methods approved by search engines, such as the practice of building relevant content and improving the quality of the site.
2. Black Hat. They resort to tricks such as camouflaging the actual content of the page, and the practice of spamming search engines.

SEO strategies have the mission of improving both the quantity of visits and the quality of visitors, where quality refers to the result of the visit to the site. This is when visitors complete the action expected by the website owner, such as buying, subscribing, learning something.

SEO has the power to attract more and more qualified visitors to a website without the need for investment in advertising and marketing.

14.1 How to become an SEO manager?

There are several paths to take if you decide to become an SEO. You can choose to be a professional who focuses on optimizing websites for on-page search engines, or who aims to improve the internal structure of a website and there are professionals who decide to work with local SEO.

Not forgetting SEO copywriters, keyword strategists, SEO checking, etc.

To become an authority and make money with SEO, you need to develop a whole set of minimum requirements, including advanced knowledge:

- Understand how search engines work.
- Know the main CMS, Content Management System, such as WordPress, Joomla, Magento, Drupal and their ideal configurations. This is because this system must have resources to improve the findability of content and be integrated with campaign management systems.
- Master the leading web analytics software, Google Analytics.
- Know everything from Excel.
- Understand the main keyword research tools, such as Google Keyword Planner, Semrush and Ahrfes.

In addition to these knowledge requirements, the SEO specialist, in order to present himself as such, must have a portfolio of success stories that helps a lot in the negotiation phase with potential clients.

Although there are many ways to specialize and make money with SEO, good experience in the field makes all the difference in understanding where to focus attention.

14.2   Duties of the SEO Analyst.

In the current scenario of companies going digital and digital marketing, the career of the professional SEO analyst is one of the ones that has the best potential remuneration in the job market, precisely due to its importance in modern digital marketing.

One of the factors that contributes to this appreciation is the degree and complexity of the attributions inherent to this specialization and the incessant updating to which this professional is subject to keep up to date with the technologies that emerge all the time.

Another factor is the constant updating of the algorithms used by large search engines such as Google.

The SEO analyst needs to be always up to date with the updates of these algorithms.

Among the duties of the SEO analyst are:

- Analysis of the website to adapt it to the requirements of search engine techniques.
- Elaboration of the strategic planning of the client's brand in the organic search environment.
- Optimization of pages and other elements of the website, such as images, videos and other digital elements considered as part of the website ranking process.
- Design and implementation of the client's website relationship with other digital elements such as websites and social media to promote the popularity of the website through link building techniques.
- Structuring of the website to adapt it to the requirements of website optimization techniques.
- Monitoring and analysis of the positions on the answer pages of the major search engines such as Google and the production of management reports on the performance of the site.

Due to the various dimensions involved in the work of an SEO analyst, this professional needs to have a broad view of all aspects of digital marketing, to be able to integrate them in order to enhance the results of the process of optimizing websites for search engines.

14.3   Learning Path to Becoming an SEO Analyst

Due to the variety and diversity of knowledge required, the training of the SEO analyst cannot be restricted solely and exclusively to the rules and techniques of website optimization, but must be comprehensive and constantly updated.

The training of the SEO professional begins with a good SEO course that contemplates not only the rules of optimization, but also the way of thinking about SEO.

The student needs to develop an understanding of the website optimization process as a whole and not just as a watertight part of the strategy in a digital marketing plan.

The student needs to develop an understanding of consumer behavior and their acquisition journey on the brand's website.

In addition, you need to intuit the processes involved and the positioning of the work developed in the conversion funnel created to obtain the desired result.

The student should get into the habit of closely following the reference sites at the moment, such as Search Engine Journal, the MOZ blog and Search Engine Land.

It is interesting for the student to practice the techniques on their own platform, such as their own blog, to experience the day-to-day work. Experience is essential for structuring a solid and successful career.

14.4   Reasons for a company to hire an SEO.

No matter the size of a business venturing into the digital world, it must have an SEO. The advantages of having this professional in the company are:

1. Democratization of access to users and visitors.
2. Getting more traffic to the client's website.
3. Consolidation of qualified traffic on the page.
4. Increased brand authority, whether organic or paid.
5. Assistance in the purchase funnel.
6. Continuous, long-term returns.
7. Improved conversion rate.

14.5   **ADVANTAGES and disadvantages of being an SEO MANAGER.**

Advantages:

- An active SEO community composed of professionals from the most varied segments, such as journalists and copywriters present in all social networks in the world.
- SEO and the SEO professional are always evolving.
- SEO helps people and businesses become better and more profitable.
- The work of analyzing data and measuring results is very rewarding and is a constant challenge.

Disadvantages:

- The result doesn't always depend solely on your work.
- Hiring an SEO isn't cheap.
- Results may take time.
- Explaining the activity of an SEO is not trivial.
- SEO alone doesn't work miracles for the company.

15 FORM 13 - PAID TRAFFIC MANAGER.

To win a number of businesses that will ensure its survival, it needs to invest in advertising on social media, which is where potential consumers spend most of their time.

Not to mention the growing number of digital influencers who want to sell their products but don't know how to work with ad platforms.

Figure 46 – The traffic manager has a lot of responsibility.

So, as it could not be otherwise, the vacancies for paid traffic manager increase day by day. There are managers who already have more than 100 clients in their portfolio!

The main task of a traffic manager is to monitor the browsing habits of Internet users and encourage them to visit a website or download an application.

To successfully fulfill their mission, traffic managers must be able to put themselves in consumers' shoes and predict reactions to online promotional campaigns.

Managers follow a cycle of procedures to help them do their jobs and constantly improve their choices of ads and digital slots.

They start by devising a sales demo plan to attract potential customers or users.

They construct their message and select the media or social networks where the ads will be displayed. The demo plan varies based on a predefined budget and sales objectives (such as the number of sales) and the average value per customer.

They will then implement the plan on social media and search engines before starting to analyze how successful it is. After this analysis, they can identify areas of improvement for the next campaign.

Finally, throughout the entire process, they must track, analyze, and understand their company's customers and the future customers they can reach. Keeping up with other media and advertising campaigns is essential to fulfill the missions of a traffic manager.

"Monitoring means putting yourself in the shoes of customers or web users. That means actively using any apps or websites that can be visited every day to see the ads."

The training of a traffic manager can be based on a university degree, business school, studies in marketing and communication, or even be self-taught – the paths to a traffic manager position are varied, as it is a relatively new profession.

Obtaining at least a two-year degree is a plus, however. Training in digital communication or even marketing is the best way to develop the primary skills needed for this job.

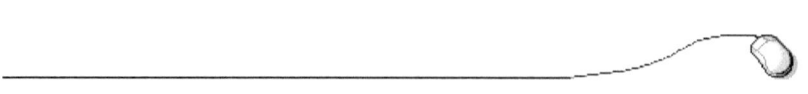

The skills required for this position are an excellent understanding of web and marketing culture, comfort in working with numbers and SEO, and an affinity for any challenge.

Traffic managers must understand not only BackOffice's tracking and advertising tools, but also users and their likely reactions to advertising plugs.

Managers are organized, love analytics, and observe their actions with a critical eye to constantly improve their advertising campaigns and monitor online ad campaigns to understand how customers behave and why they buy.

A traffic manager works with the sales teams and the communications department. They act as the liaison between consumers and the company.

While this varies from company to company, traffic managers are usually attached to the marketing department and report to the marketing director.

They may also be part of a traffic acquisition team, under the supervision of a procurement manager.

One possibility for advancement as a traffic manager is to take on more managerial responsibilities as the head of a team of traffic managers. Other options are for sales or marketing manager positions. Some traffic managers also choose to become consultants.

Among the functions and responsibilities of the traffic manager, we can mention:

- Manage advertising on your clients' online platforms, such as Face-book Ads, Google Ads, Bing Ads, LinkedIn Ads, Pinterest Ads, TikTok Ads, Taboola, Outbrain, etc.
- Track conversion rates.
- Increase online sales and leverage the client's business.
- Make your brand better known,
- Create the ads and paid campaigns on digital platforms.
- Manage the budget allocated to marketing campaigns.
- Run A/B tests on campaigns.
- Produce reports periodically with analysis of the results.
- Create actions on Landing Pages and website access, for example.
- Define the budget for the campaigns with the directors and presidents.
- Attract new customers to the company.

The traffic manager can work both as an employee and as a service provider without an employment relationship. In the latter case, this professional may have several clients simultaneously.

To act as a paid traffic manager, it is essential to have not only mastery of the tools, but also to have mastery of persuasive writing techniques (copywriting) and aptitude with numbers to make the financial management of campaign investments.

This professional is, in general, hired by communication agencies, marketing and celebrities in the digital world who invest in ads on the internet, either for the launch of a product in the market or for traffic management of perpetual products.

To win a significant number of customers, it is essential that he presents results, demonstrates how and how much his management contributes to the success and sale of his customers' products and services.

It is worth noting that there is a difference between the manager and the paid traffic analyst, even if these functions are performed by only one professional. In addition to creating ads on the platforms, the traffic manager is also responsible for the strategic part of the business itself.

He needs to have mastery of the business and the client's growth objectives as a whole to be able to create the strategic plan for the campaigns. In addition, it may also be responsible for managing the analysts.

The traffic analyst, in turn, is the professional who will take care of the effective creation of ads on the platforms.

15.1 Why have a traffic manager in the company?

The answer to this question is very simple. The paid traffic manager has the potential to:

- Increase the company's sales.
- Prospect new customers.
- Reduce expenses of a physical business.
- In some cases, it serves customers from diverse geographic locations.
- It broadens a company's horizons by exploring new markets and opportunities.

If you still haven't had the opportunity to stop to think about how important traffic is for your brand, it's a good idea to know the subject, as it is considered one of the enablers of your company's digital business structure since it generates new customers, followers, readers, or whatever your intention is by attracting visits to your website and allows the diagnosis of the performance of organizations' marketing actions.

The audience that enters and leaves your pages says everything about your positioning and brand in the market and in relation to the competition. The analysis of this traffic allows you to understand what you did wrong or what you got right in your planning.

There are two types of traffic: organic and paid. Paid traffic is earned by advertising or contracted and paid ads. It is this type that needs to be monitored so that the results are maximized.

An example, with regard to the current technology of accessing websites, is the paid and served banners. That is, you create a campaign and pay for the placement. It can be a fixed amount or with a cost only when the user clicks on the ad. The layout of your banner on the contracted website has the following possibilities:

Some companies have a certain distrust regarding the result of banners, but it is a guaranteed way to accelerate the results of advertising campaigns. The question is how to distribute the messages in a way that results in business.

Obtaining the planned result in companies' advertising campaigns is based on planning focused on the relationship with their audience. This relationship should be treated as a focal point, it is necessary that you know your PERSONA, your target audience, and promote your best experience. With this, it is important to:

- Create a content plan to be published.
- Create a media plan.
- Identify which campaigns will be boosted.
- Select the campaigns in which advertising pieces will be created.

15.2   Classification of traffic managers?

The classification of traffic managers considers where it will operate and the type of traffic that will be managed.

1. Instagram traffic manager.

An Instagram traffic manager analyzes and organizes all the marketing potential that the tool offers, such as:

- The promotion of ads for specific posts.
- The generation of free content.
- Partnerships with other brands.
- Sweepstakes and various promotions.

2. Traffic manager for facebook ads.

The traffic manager in the Face-book Ads tool must plan, manage and direct the resources applied in paid advertising campaigns that intend to reach their consumers on this social network.

The challenges are several, but the main ones are to be able to deal with the audience that comes from a variety of backgrounds, determine how much money to use, and align engagement plans to this audience profile.

3. Traffic manager for google ads.

Google Ads is a real challenge for an institutional website to reach the first pages of Google. It is necessary to do structural engineering within the pages, involving text, layout and programming, using an SEO plan.

A Google Ads traffic manager needs to know how to control the cost of a paid campaign in detail so that the company is highlighted at the top of the page in the form of an ad.

4. Social media management.

The social media landscape is not trivial to manage. There is a whole set of techniques around social media management.

Having the ability to measure the type of content, frequency of posts, knowledge of the consumer audience, the algorithms that determine how users interact, and how this content will be delivered, can make the company stand out or "burn its film" among the competition or in front of the potential consumer.

The problem isn't just posting a piece of content. True expertise is the one that uses all the techniques and knowledge to put one company ahead of another.

It is, at the end of the day, the difference between getting people's attention and losing it. The social media manager needs to have differentiated skills and use them wisely.

15.3 How Much Does a Paid Traffic Manager Make?

The traffic manager has two forms of remuneration:

- A percentage of sales made.
- A fixed salary.

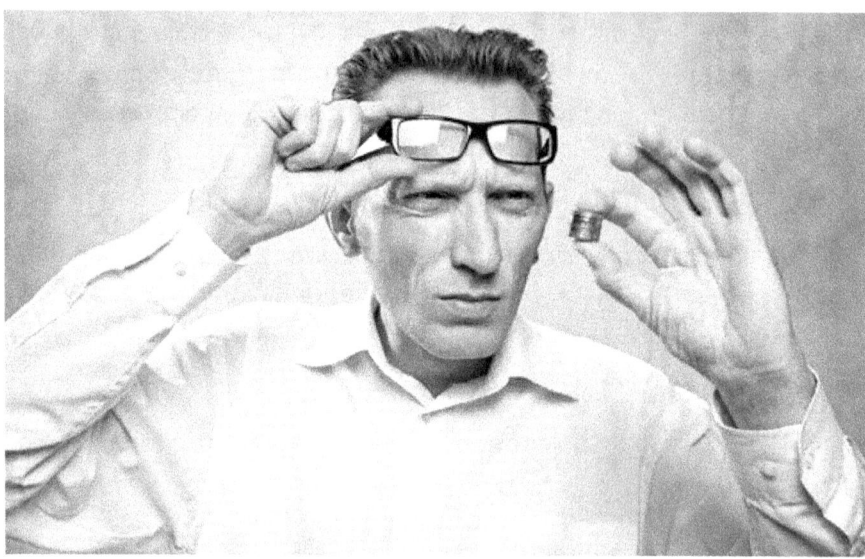
Figure 47 "And the salary, oh!

The salary range[15] of the Traffic Manager is between R$ 3,000.00, the median salary of the survey, and the salary ceiling of R$ 12,182.19, with R$ 4,581.23 being the average of the 2022 salary floor of collective agreements taking into account professionals under the CLT regime[16] throughout Brazil.

The city with the most occurrences of hiring and, consequently, with the most job vacancies for Traffic Manager is São Paulo - SP.

---

[15] October 2022 values.
[16] The acronym CLT stands for Consolidation of Labor Laws and is nothing more than a set of laws that serve to regulate labor relations and protect workers. These are the rights and duties of employees and employers.

16 FORMA 14 - COPYWRITER.

A copywriter creates clear and compelling copy to sell products and/or educate and engage consumers by exercising the power of persuasive writing on websites, blog posts, product descriptions, email blasts, banner ads, newsletters, white papers, PSAs, social media platforms including Twitter and Instagram, and other marketing communication vehicles.

The job may also involve brainstorming concepts and developing storyboards[17], working with marketing and other creative departments to develop communication strategies, and ensuring consistent brand messaging, including voice and tone, across print, TV, radio, direct mail, and other communication channels.

A typical workday might include researching a topic online or conducting an interview, figuring out how to convey an idea to a specific audience, writing and editing copy, and finding images to accompany the content.

A copywriter is someone who writes for the internet. They create informative content for businesses that is designed to guide the reader's own search.

16.1   What skills are needed?

Writing skills, of course! But we're talking about more than the ability to put together a coherent sentence. "As a professional, you need to know how to write copy that sells to the specific audience of the client, agency, or company."

Grammar, spelling, and punctuation also count. Spelling can make or break your career.

The ability to write for any audience and superior research skills are also crucial, as is meeting deadlines.

---

[17] The storyboard is a sequence of frame-by-frame drawings with the outline of scenes designed for video content, such as films and animations.

Figure 48 – Essential skills of a Copywriter.

If you can't deliver quality content in a certain timeframe, you probably won't be able to as a copywriter.

Lastly, you have to be able to follow the instructions. This is especially true for freelancers hired to listen to what someone is looking for and execute that vision. A copywriter's job is to provide made-to-order products.

Writing content is no longer enough. You need to know how to optimize content to drive traffic to your client's website, landing page,[18] or blog.

This means staying up-to-date with digital technology, including Google's algorithm changes, so you know which SEO techniques are most effective.

16.2   How can one enter this field?

A bachelor's degree in something like journalism, English, or marketing can help, but a powerful portfolio filled with a variety of samples you've created for online writing classes or internships or while providing your services to a nonprofit is what will impress potential employers.

---

[18] A Landing Page is a page that has all the elements aimed at conversion, from the visitor to the Lead or from the opportunity to the customer. Also known as landing pages, conversion pages, or capture pages, they are a key item in Digital Marketing campaigns. Here's everything you need to know about them.

The career path to becoming a copywriter is not rigid – there are many ways to get started and build your resume. Here are a few different things you can do to make it easier to get a writing job:

1. Study advertising, communication, or writing in school.

Even if you don't plan on getting a formal education in copywriting, a simple writing class or writing course in high school or college can teach you a lot about what great copy looks like.

A writing course should teach you how to develop your writing style, how to understand the mechanics of the English language, and how to recognize the cultural implications of each word.

2. Start small.

Even if you don't have a single writing job, don't lose hope. It's common for small businesses or local business owners to hire freelance writers with little experience.

Doing some of these copywriting jobs for beginners can help you get the experience you need – not to mention building a contact list of potential clients for the future.

3. Build your copywriting portfolio.

If you're a copywriter trying to get a job in advertising, your portfolio is the best opportunity to showcase how you write. Think of it as your sales page, where you advertise your copywriting services to potential clients. In your writing samples, be expressive.

Have a personality. Make sure you use proper grammar and check the spelling of your work. Show that you are capable of writing headlines and that you can create compelling copy that captures the attention of even the most disinterested customer.

If you don't have any examples of writing you've done for paying clients, get creative: start your own blog or assign yourself some copy prompts for fun to fill out your portfolio or even impress a specific business.

4. Learn and keep up with SEO trends.

The main challenge of marketing is getting ads and content seen by the right people. That's why search engine optimization (SEO) is important.

SEO is a strategic approach to content creation that makes it more searchable online – meaning you're more likely to appear above other competitor pages when a relevant word is searched.

SEO rules are always changing and can include keyword usage, word count, specific content formats, and more, so learning how to write for SEO and keeping up with current trends will make it more marketable to businesses.

But remember that SEO isn't everything – if you want to win over a reader, you'll still have to write compelling copy.

16.3   What do copywriters write?

The kind of things they write include:

1. Blog posts. These can range from around 400 to 1500 words. They are usually a bit more informal or opinionated, but this varies from client to client.
2. White Papers. But not like the ones in the government. White papers tend to be 1,500 to 2,500 words long and are informative and educational documents that explain the origins of a problem and how it can be solved. Often, this solution will be tied to what the customer sells, but most of the white paper will be objective and useful. These tend to be locked behind a form and are used for lead capture.
3. Emails. Email campaigns exist to pique interest, raise awareness, and spur action. They need to be short, compelling, and informative to help nurture leads into customers.
4. Social media posts. Those limited-character tweets and witty Facebook updates don't write themselves, you know. Social media also requires copyright.
5. Case studies. These are short articles that explain how a company has helped its customers. Case studies often have a formulaic structure, but a good copywriter can find the story within it.

6. Industry reports. Sometimes we have to go heavy and write some hardcore reports. These are based on real research that expands on a particular subject, industry, or trend.
7. Website Copy. Writing for the web comes with its own set of rules and guiding principles. It's a whole other skill set, but a lot of copywriters have it up their sleeves.

16.4   How Much Does a Copywriter Make?

A CLT Copywriter or freelancer at the beginning of their career can earn from $1,500 to $10,000 per month.

Taking into account that the minimum wage in 2022 is R$1,200.00, a beginner Copywriter, who works on a single project, already starts earning more than 33.8 million Brazilians with a monthly income of up to one minimum wage.

Thus, if you want to work in traditional companies and agencies, fulfill your 44 hours a week, working from Monday to Friday, the average salary that companies pay for Copywriters in Brazil is R$ 4,092.00, according to Glassdoor[19].

But even as a CLT Copywriter it is possible to go further and make a lot more money with words.

---

[19] October 2022 values.

17 FORM 15 - IMAGE EDITING.

Image editing refers to the modification or enhancement of digital or traditional photographic images using different techniques, tools, or software. Images produced by scanners, digital cameras, or other image-capturing devices may be good, but not perfect.

Figure 49 – Image editing requires professional software.

Image editing is done to create the best possible look for the images and also to improve the overall quality of the image according to different parameters.

An image editor works with designers and other editors to create a complete and rich experience for the reader or client.

As an image editor, you can work in a wide range of industries, including news, book publishing, advertising, website development, and the arts.

You may be asked to retouch photos for advertising or select and edit images to accompany a story. You can work with photographers to discuss the goals of a project and collaborate to achieve it.

17.1   What skills does a photo editor need?

Creativity and a well-trained eye are important. As well as being a solid foundation in photography and art history.

No one expects you to be a professional photographer, but it helps to have a basic understanding of color balance, lighting and even some filmmaking techniques, says Lange, whose job is to determine which of Shutterstock's 90 million images best represents a project.

You'll also need attention to detail and organizational skills to overcome the logistical challenges that will inevitably arise when producing even the smallest photo shoot, she adds.

Figure 50 – The photo editor is not a photographer, but it works miracles.

Although photo editors aren't actually taking the photos, they need to know everything there is to know about photography. They must have good business sense (to negotiate contracts), and it is imperative that they have extensive contacts within the industry. That's because they need to know what type of photographer will be the best for each particular shoot.

For example, if the shoot requires multiple photographs of a family, this will likely require a family portrait photographer which is quite different from a beauty shoot of a consumer product like shampoo.

A consumer product photo is very different from a high-fashion photograph that will appear next to a story about Chanel.

Also, while you may know the best fashion photographer in the business, they may be hired on another task, so you need a large arsenal of names to use.

17.2   What about digital skills?

"Photoshop and InDesign skills are especially useful for making minor corrections yourself or for better understanding the needs of the art department," Lange continues. Experience with Illustrator, other photo editing software like Lightroom and Bridge, and some knowledge of videography and video editing are the icing on the cake.

17.3   Who is the supervisor of a photo editor?

It depends on the organization, but you'll likely receive guidance from an art or cinematographer.

17.4   What does it take to excel in this position?

A deep-rooted passion for photography and the industry in general, for starters. As with most jobs, liking what you do shows up in your work, and this show is no different.

And flexibility. Sometimes, your concept can leave the editors and designers you work with scratching their heads. Be willing to reevaluate (or change) your view when necessary.

17.5   A precious tip.

Keep an eye on photographers and their portfolios, particularly emerging photographers and developing trends in the industry, advises Lange.

17.6   How can I enter this field?

Many employers require a bachelor's degree in photojournalism, visual arts, photography, or a similar field to be a photo editor.

You should develop your knowledge and skill of equipment over time and compile a portfolio of your best work.

You'll need a strong working knowledge of editing programs such as Adobe Lightroom, Photoshop, and InDesign.

A strong portfolio will be valuable in getting your first photo editor job and starting your career in this field.

17.7   Advantages of photo editing for businesses.

With the rise of image-centric social networks such as Instagram and Pinterest, photos are quickly becoming a universal marketing language. People always relate better to visual cues, and if you're in the food, fashion, retail, or travel industry, professionally edited images should be at the top of the list when it comes to your marketing initiatives. Let's look at 8 key benefits of photo editing for your business needs –

1. Brand building.

Images are extremely important for building your brand. Businesses can focus on a specific style of editing, such as focusing on specific color saturation, crop pattern, nature of images, subjects used, focus patterns, etc., to create an edited image with brand recognition. This also leads to better customer recall for your business offerings, ensuring that they feel more confident when purchasing your product or service

2. Best sales.

The very essence of photo editing is to increase the overall quality of your images. Businesses don't want mediocre images to represent their products or services.

Good photo editors can instantly change the look and quality of an image to make it appealing to the general public, one of the best examples of this can be found in fast-food marketing and with brands like McDonald's etc.

3. Build respectability and credibility.

One of the main benefits of photo editing, especially for businesses that are just starting out, is the way it can help a business gain credibility in a tough market.

About 46% of people find it easier to trust a company that shows genuine images on their website, compared to stock images.

By editing your photos in a professional manner, a small office can look spacious and inviting, without misleading your viewers

4. Photo-intensive tasks become easier.

In cases where your business relies heavily on product photography and images, such as e-commerce sites, etc., you need to ensure a steady stream of high-quality images on a daily basis.

67% of consumers believe that the overall quality of a product's image is "extremely important" to them selecting and purchasing a product.

Photo editing makes it easy to set the exact editing parameters and later apply the same settings to other images, thus reducing your effort. Similarly, if you have multiple similar images, you can quickly process them by grouping them together and applying preset editing settings

5. Robust social media strategy.

Today, social media is the primary marketing channel for most businesses out there. From Facebook to Instagram, and many others, social media has managed to bring customers and brands closer together than ever before.

By professionally editing your images before uploading, adding visual cues, beautiful word art, etc., you can give your business an edge over the competition

6. Reuse Images for Better Efficiency

Reusing images for various purposes is one of the advantages of photo editing. With the help of professional photo editing tools, you can use the same image for various purposes by changing its background or beating it with other images.

This, in turn, helps you streamline your processes efficiently and focus on other aspects of your marketing plan

7. Easy cross-platform customization

The appearance of an image in your print ads may be different from your digital ads; It can be different for social media, for mobile platforms, for monochrome prints, etc.

Only with the help of professional photo editing, you can customize your images to have the same impact on multiple platforms

8. Other Advantages

From compressing large-sized images into smaller images for faster web page loading to resizing and cropping, there are many other advantages of photo editing for businesses.

Even if you only work with print media, you earn by editing your photos according to the requirements of the media and the consumers who read it, leading to highly effective targeted advertising.

17.8   Salary Range & Salary Floor 2022[20]

The Image Editor's salary range is between R$ 2,749.00, the median salary of the survey, and the salary ceiling of R$ 8,333.94, with R$ 3,468.25 being the average of the 2022 salary floor of collective agreements taking into account professionals under the CLT regime throughout Brazil.

The most recurrent professional profile is that of a 25-year-old male worker who works 44 hours a week in companies in the Temporary Labor Rental segment.

---

[20] October 2022 values.

The city with the most occurrences of hiring and, consequently, with the most job vacancies for Image Editor is São Paulo - SP.

18 FORM 16 - SALE OF PHOTOGRAPHS.

Whether you're a professional photographer or just enjoy taking photos in your spare time, you can earn a decent amount by selling your photos online – even without a high-end camera. In fact, if you have a decent camera and a steady hand, you've already got a chance.

Regardless of how you take your photos, there are a growing number of ways to monetize the photos you've already taken. And there are plenty of other ways to develop your photography skills (and income), from selling your Insta stash to creating a photo book.

Before you start making money by selling your photos online, it's important to get good photography equipment. But as we said earlier, you don't have to spend a fortune on a fancy camera to sell your images.

If you have a DSLR camera (or like to buy one for a swipe), you'll have more options for selling photos to stock libraries, to print sites, or to print-on-demand products. This is because digital cameras often produce high-resolution images.

However, some smartphones are outperforming digital cameras these days, such as the Samsung Galaxy S22 Ultra and Google Pixel 6 Pro.

An increasing number of websites are buying photos taken on mobile phones, so research which stock photo site is best for you.

18.1   How to sell photos online through image libraries.

Stock libraries buy and sell digital photos to use on websites, books, products, and even in advertisements, with the photographer receiving a cut of the sale each time.

Selling photos through a stock website is a great way to browse passive income ideas: you can upload a photo once and sell it multiple times, pretty much forever!

You may have to submit a selection of photos (and be accepted) before you can become a contributor to an online photo library. After that, some sites will continue to review all of your submissions and gladly reject any that they feel don't meet the standards.

This means that you'll always need to be on the ball to pick your best shots. However, don't be too worried about rejections – join several stock image sites and post photos on all of them to get the best coverage possible.

18.2   Best sites to sell your photos online.

To make as much money as possible selling photos online, try these image sites:

1. Alamy.

I recommend trying Alamy first to start selling photos. On average, images on Alamy sell for around £65 each, but photos can cost anywhere from £15 to £360, depending on the use of your photos.

Selling phone photos through the Stockimo app (App Store only) guarantees a 20% reduction.

2. Picfair.

Picfair has an important differentiator: you decide how much your images are sold for. Of course, the lower you set the price, the more likely people are to buy your images.

But, if you have some high-quality photos that deserve high prices, this site is ideal.

Picfair adds 20%, but the selling price you set is what you get if your image sells.

3. EyeEm.

If Instagram and Alamy had a loving child, it would be like EyeEm. EyeEm is a photo-sharing site, but if you want to earn more than 'likes', you can also sell your images through the marketplace.

You would earn between 25% and 55% of image sales, depending on how much money you made from the site last year.

As a bonus, on EyeEm there are also regular how-to articles and themed missions carried out by big brands. Also, you can upload photos via the web or phone.

4. Foap.

Foap is built around phone photographers, with everything handled through the app (free on Android and the App Store).

Foap sells photos for around £7 – £8 and splits them 50/50 after reductions of any taxes and fees.

They also run regular quests where you can submit photos on a theme for a chance to earn extra money and perks.

5. Dreamstime.

Dreamstime offers up to 60% for exclusive contributors.

The value of your photo also increases the more it is downloaded: beginner images can sell for around £0.25 to £3.50.

If you're selling photos taken on a phone, start with the free Dreamstime app (on Android and iPhone).

6. Imagens Getty.

Getty Images delivers 15% of an image's selling price, but promises a bigger crop if you make the image site-exclusive (about 25% – 45%!).

Single images are sold from £50, but the type of licence or subscription plan the customer buys determines how their slice is calculated.

7. Shutterstock.

Shutterstock is one of the most well-known image sites for selling. The amount you'll earn per photo depends on the type of license or subscription, as well as your lifetime earnings (the total amount you've earned on Shutterstock as a contributor).

It's worth noting that you'll only earn 15% per image sold when you start as a Shutterstock contributor.

The more you sell in a year, the higher the percentage you'll receive. But, at the beginning of each calendar year, this resets and you'll go back to earning 15% per image until you sell more again.

18.3   Tips to make extra money selling photos.

Here are the best ways to make more money selling photos online.

1. Upload quality images to various stock photo sites.
2. Include people in your photos – but it's worth noting that anyone you date may need to sign a model release form to say they agree to you using it. Your stock library will have template forms that you can print, sign, and send.
3. Check the T&Cs before selling photos to stock photography sites, including when you'll get paid, how much, and in what currency. Also, find out what happens to your photos if you want to cancel your account later. You may find that you could make more money selling to a different stock library.
4. Sign up for photo site contributor newsletters to get information on what photos are in demand and how to improve your camera and editing skills.
5. Use relevant keywords when uploading photos to image sites, as this will help more people find (and buy!) them!).

18.4   How to Sell Your Photos as Prints

Before you head over to Boots to batch print your vacation photos, there's a little more to it than that. While you can sell photos printed on your home printer or in a street lab, better quality images yield higher profits.

This means using a suitable print lab (which specializes in framed art or prints), opting for specialized paper, or even selling limited or signed editions.

There is a lot of freedom in selling photographic prints. You decide what to shoot, who to sell it to, and for how much. And, like selling through stock libraries, it can be a good source of passive income.

18.5 Use a photo hosting site

Photographer-friendly website hosts give you a secure place to store your digital photos, a portfolio (so you can show them off), and shopping tools (so you can sell prints, downloads, and wall art).

They even handle the print and any postage every time you make a sale. Sounds great, right?

There's a catch, though—not only do they charge for hosting your website, but they also take a cheeky cut of every sale—and that's not everyone's cup of cocoa. If you want to give it a try, look for free trials before you spend the money: try Zenfolio or Smugmug.

Open an online photo shop

Alternatively, you can always start your own website or Etsy shop and keep more of your profit.

Making prints or gifts to sell is also super simple – opt for print-on-demand and you won't have to store any inventory (or run out of pocket if you can't sell it).

18.6 Sell photos on social media

Take a cue from the students who earn from your review when you post your study notes on Instagram. Obviously, it helps if you already have a large following online, but if you have talent (and the right hashtags), you have a chance to make money.

As an example of a way to make money on social media, you can take photos of some products that you would recommend to your followers and then share them with affiliate links on sites like Instagram, Twitter, and Facebook.

19 FORM 17 - ONLINE PRIVATE TUTOR.

For several years, the main role of the teacher was simply to share knowledge, since they were considered the sole holders of information.

However, little by little, people realized that the participation of everyone involved in the teaching and learning process was very beneficial.

With this interaction, students can share their own experiences and knowledge and the teacher's role is also to mediate the discussions generated in the educational environment.

With distance education (EAD), this role is no different.

There is a belief that the role of the teacher is not that important in teaching on the web. But the truth is that it is fundamental: uniting knowledge, technology and students.

Thanks to modern technology, students of all ages can use the internet to connect with teachers from the comfort of their own homes. While online tutoring can mean a variety of different things, it's basically providing one-on-one learning support to students over the internet.

Private tutors work with students as early as kindergarten, but primarily serve elementary through high school students, college students, and adult learners through a distance learning format.

These professionals reinforce the subject matter and provide feedback using positive reinforcement to motivate, encourage, and build confidence in students.

Some private tutors work with students to improve their study skills, while others may help clients improve their note-taking or testing skills.

Private tutors review class material, help solve problems, and go over assignments with students. Depending on the employer, some private tutors are responsible for scheduling instructional activities, grading student work, and monitoring student performance.

Private teacher training programs are available in both classrooms and online and typically cover areas such as cultural awareness, listening strategies, and building businesses for self-employed private tutors.

Some online tutors choose to be professionally accredited or certified by agencies such as the National Tutoring Association or the American Tutoring Association.

19.1 What Are The Qualifications For An Online Private Tutoring Job?

Private tutors are usually experts in the subject they teach. Most employers require a minimum four-year degree to work as a private tutor, but many require more than that. In some cases, college students get private tutoring jobs online.

Most private tutors hold teaching certificates and master's degrees. Some employers require a Ph.D. Classroom teaching experience or a state-issued teaching credential is sometimes required.

The skills you need to succeed as an online tutor include:

- Active listening.
- Reading comprehension.
- Learning strategies.

19.2 What technology is needed to work as an online tutor?

Innovative technology has transformed the private tutoring profession over the past decade. Students and private tutors can interact from anywhere in the world at any time, and private tutors can share documents and other resources with students instantly using online tools.

At a minimum, online tutors should have a reliable personal computer or laptop, high-speed internet, and a webcam.

Depending on the employer, online tutors will use various online tools to communicate and share resources with their students.

Most private tutors use some form of computer-based training, email, and spreadsheet software, and probably use some form of database user interface and query software.

Online tools commonly used by online tutors include:

- Skype.
- White board.
- Microsoft Office.
- Google Drive.
- Wikispaces.

19.3 What is the profile of the online private tutor?

People who are interested in teaching students online often share an interest in helping people, talking, and teaching.

Other attributes of great private tutors include being reliable and cooperative, having integrity, self-control and concern for others, and paying close attention to detail.

Online classes offer great flexibility and the opportunity to work from home. While some private tutors work full-time, most online tutors enjoy flexible, part-time schedules.

19.4 How Much Does a Private Tutor Make.

To give you an idea, we can observe the average amount charged by private teachers in all areas of knowledge around 100 reais.

Let's imagine, for example, that you manage to teach four classes per week, that is, 1,600.00 reais per month.

20 FORMA 18 – DROPSHIPPING.

Let's start our list with one of the most popular ways to make money online. According to Google Trends, the popularity of dropshipping is increasing, highlighting its viability as a business idea.

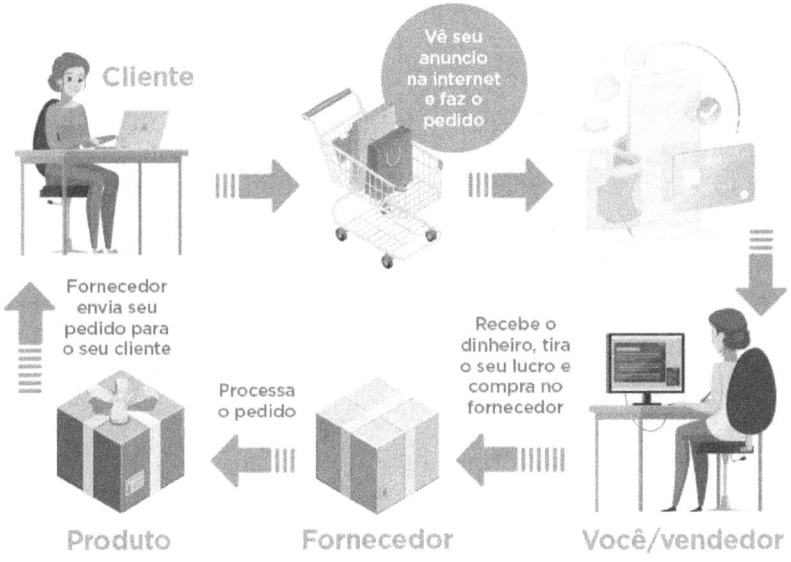

Figure 51 - The dropshipping cycle.

With success stories about how an entrepreneur made $6,667 in eight weeks or how a store owner made six figures selling just one product, there's plenty of proof that dropshipping is a real way to make money online.

Dropshipping is a business model where you sell a product to a customer, but the supplier stores, packages, and ships the product to your customers on your behalf.

With dropshipping, you have access to millions of products that you can add to your store. Some Shopify dropshipping apps allow you to handpick your product images, edit item descriptions, and give your business a personalized vibe, so people will love shopping with you.

The best way to make money with dropshipping?

Most entrepreneurs have focused on a few marketing strategies:

- Running Facebook ads.
- Have influencers promote your products.
- Sending direct messages (DMs) to potential customers on social media.

20.1 How to Start Dropshipping in 7 Steps

Many people start their dropshipping business during their time off from their day jobs. Here's a step-by-step plan.

1. Choose a niche and your initial products. Find something to sell that people want. You can see trending product listings on sites like Oberlo, check Google Trends, browse other sites in a niche that interests you. Choose products that you're enthusiastic about selling, but remember that no niche will work if it's not profitable.
2. Analyze the competition. Learn the business. Google shows you who is at the top of your chosen niche. You want to know who your competitors are, what and how they sell, and what they're doing right or wrong. Check their marketing and pricing. Also, read about the eCommerce business. Learn from the experiences of others.
3. Find suppliers. If you don't have one in mind yet, you can check out online dropshipping supplier directories. Please contact your list for information on your minimum orders and shipping times. Place sample orders to compare product quality and packaging.
4. Choose a name and develop a brand concept. Think about your products and your buyers. Identify your potential customers and consider what appeals to them. Your domain name is your first impression, so choose carefully.
5. Create your dropshipping website. Follow your brand's concept and make it look professional. Create content and a customer experience that drives sales.
6. Market. Market. Market. This is your most important task. Do more of Step 2 and get creative.
7. Analyze and improve. Then do it again. Use good analytical tools because data is key. Guesswork can sometimes lead to success, but do you really want to trust it?

20.2 How to Create a Dropshipping Website

1. Choose a rich platform for your eCommerce website.
2. Create your layout or choose a template that you can customize.
3. Make your customer's experience special, memorable, and targeted to your audience.
4. Create branded cart and checkout experiences.
5. When you're ready, start selling!

20.3 Benefits of dropshipping

Here are some other reasons why dropshipping is such a popular eCommerce business model for businesses large and small.

1. Less start-up capital required.

Probably the biggest advantage of dropshipping is that it's possible to launch an eCommerce store without having to invest thousands of dollars in inventory. Traditionally, a brick-and-mortar or e-commerce retailer needs to tie up large amounts of capital purchase inventory.

With the dropshipping model, you don't have to buy a product unless you've already made the sale and been paid by the customer. Without significant upfront investments in inventory, it is possible to start dropshipping and succeed with very little money.

Additionally, since you're not committed to selling through any inventory purchased upfront like with other business models, there's less risk involved in starting a dropshipping store.

2. Easy to get started.

Running an eCommerce business is much easier when you don't have to deal with physical products. With dropshipping, you don't have to worry about:

- Managing or paying for a warehouse.
- Packing and shipping your orders.
- Inventory tracking for accounting reasons.
- Handling returns and inbound shipments.
- Order products continuously and manage the stock level.

3. Low overload.

Since you don't have to deal with purchasing inventory or managing distribution centers, your overhead is quite low.

In fact, many successful dropshipping stores are run as home-based businesses, requiring little more than a laptop and a few recurring expenses to operate.

As you grow, these costs will likely increase, but they will still be low compared to traditional brick-and-mortar businesses.

4. Flexible location.

With dropshipping, a successful business can be run from almost anywhere with an internet connection.

As long as you can communicate with suppliers and provide timely service and support that meets customer expectations, you will be able to run and manage your business.

5. Wide selection of products to sell.

Since you don't have to pre-purchase the items you sell, you can offer a variety of trending products to your potential customers.

Plus, you can switch or change your dropshipping product list without having to worry about unsold inventory. If suppliers stock an item, you can put it up for sale in your online store at no additional cost.

6. Easier to test.

Dropshipping is a useful fulfillment model for both launching a new store and business owners who want to test the appetite customers have for additional product categories, for example, accessories or entirely new product lines. The main benefit of dropshipping is, again, the ability to list and potentially sell products before committing to buying a large amount of inventory.

7. Easier to scale.

With a traditional retail business, if you get three times the number of orders, you typically need to do three times as much work. By leveraging dropshipping suppliers, most of the work to process additional orders will be done by the suppliers, allowing you to expand with fewer growing pains and less incremental work.

Sales growth will always bring additional work – especially related to customer support – but businesses that utilize the scale of dropshipping are particularly good over traditional eCommerce businesses.

20.4 Disadvantages of dropshipping.

All the benefits we've mentioned make dropshipping a very attractive model for those who are just starting out with an online store or those who want to expand their existing product offerings.

But like all approaches, dropshipping also has its drawbacks. Generally speaking, convenience and flexibility come at a higher price.

Here are some shortcomings to consider when considering a dropshipping business.

1. Low profit margins.

Low margins are the biggest drawback of operating in a highly competitive dropshipping vertical. Because it's so easy to get started and because overhead costs are so minimal, many competing companies set up a dropshipping store and sell items at rock-bottom prices in an attempt to increase revenue. Because they invested so little to start the business, they can afford to operate on razor-thin margins.

Usually, these sellers will have low-quality websites and poor customer service (if any), which can help you differentiate your dropshipping business.

But that won't stop customers from comparing their prices to yours. This increase in competition will quickly hurt the potential profit margin in a niche.

Fortunately, you can do a lot to mitigate this problem by choosing the right products and selecting a niche/vertical suitable for dropshipping.

2. Inventory issues.

If you stock all of your own products, it's relatively simple to keep track of which items are in and out of stock.

But when you're buying from multiple warehouses, which are also fulfilling orders from other merchants, the inventory can change daily.

Fortunately, nowadays, there are several apps that allow you to sync with suppliers. So, dropshippers can "pass on" customer orders to a dropshipping supplier with one or two clicks and should be able to see in real-time how much inventory the supplier has.

DSers also allow merchants to take automated actions when a supplier's inventory reaches zero.

For example, when a product is no longer available, you can unpublish the product automatically, or keep the product published but automatically set the quantity to zero.

3. Shipping complexities.

If you work with multiple suppliers – like most dropshippers – the products on your online store will be sourced through a number of different dropshippers. This means that you have no control over the supply chain.

Let's say a customer place an order for three items, all of which are only available from separate vendors. You'll incur three separate shipping charges to ship each item to the customer, but it's probably not wise to pass this charge on to the customer. And even when it makes sense to include those charges, automating those drop shipping calculations can be difficult.

4. Supplier errors.

Have you ever been blamed for something that wasn't your fault, but you had to accept responsibility anyway?

Even the best dropshipping suppliers make mistakes when fulfilling orders – mistakes for which you must take responsibility and apologize. Additionally, mediocre and low-quality suppliers will hurt the customer experience through missing items, poorly made shipments, and packaging or product quality issues, which can damage your company's reputation.

5. Limited customization and branding.

Unlike custom or print-on-demand products, dropshipping doesn't give you much control over the product itself. Usually, the dropshipping product is designed and branded by the supplier.

Some dropshipping suppliers can accommodate your company's product changes. Even then, though, the supplier has more control over the product itself. Any changes or additions to the product usually require a minimum order quantity to make it viable and affordable for the manufacturer.

21 FORM 19 – PRINT ON DEMAND.

Print-on-demand (POD) is another popular way to make money online. Many people have adopted this business model because it has lower overhead expenses than other businesses.

Print on demand is similar to dropshipping in the sense that you don't have to carry inventory or ship products to customers yourself. There are two minor differences, however.

Figure 52 - The print-on-demand cycle.

First, you can create your own custom products, which is great for brand awareness. Secondly, you can choose from specific items instead of a vast array of categories.

Most print-on-demand companies offer easy-to-print products such as t-shirts, mugs, and tote bags.

The best way to make money from your print-on-demand business? Free marketing channels. Your best bet would be to promote your products for free on Instagram and Pinterest and through social media influencers who convert your audience well.

With custom products, you can start your own clothing line, monetize your audience, or cater to a specific niche. Print-on-demand is a fulfillment model that makes all of this possible without having to maintain your own inventory.

But choosing the best paid or free print-on-demand companies to work with and bring your vision to life can take a lot of research. Each platform has its own distinct catalog of products, shipping considerations, and unique features that will be factored into your decision.

To help narrow down your list of options, we've reviewed 10 of the best free and paid print-on-demand sites for designing, selling, and shipping your own custom products.

21.1   How do I start my own print-on-demand business?

Here's how print-on-demand works:

- Choose a product to sell.
- Finalize a design for your merchandise.
- Select a name for your brand.
- Select a Print Provider.
- Sign up for an eCommerce platform like Shopify.
- Set up your online store for your brand.
- Market your products.

21.2   Is print on demand profitable?

On average, brands can earn $500 per month by running a print-on-demand business.

There's always a chance to earn more if your marketing and designs reach your audience. Remember to analyze what trends your ideal customers are following.

21.3   How Do You Price Print on Demand Products?

Here's how to price print-on-demand products:

- Evaluate the cost of your product (design, production, shipping, taxes, and platform fees per order).
- Add a Profit Margin on Product Cost: Product Cost + Profit Margin = Retail Cost.
- Calculate Your Other Expenses (Marketing & Advertising): Other Monthly Costs / Your Profit Margin = Minimum Orders.
- Set a price for your product that covers all your expenses and still leaves you with a margin.

22 MEET THE AUTHOR.

22.1   Prof. Marcão - Marcus Vinícius Pinto.

Figure 53- The Value of Human Capital.

In my career, which has been marked by decades of experience in information technology and marketing, it is important to highlight my constant search for improvement and a deep understanding of information science and the complex functioning of the human mind.

Despite the challenge of living with a physical disability, more specifically the absence of the left foot, this singular fact has driven me to constantly seek to overcome and value the uniqueness of each individual.

Currently, I'm in a moment of consolidation in my career as a writer. I am deeply involved with topics related to information science and seek to bring to light an insightful and comprehensive view of the complex processes of data storage, organization, and dissemination.

Through my words, I seek to unveil the complexities of the human being and his mind in all its nuances.

During these decades, I have dedicated myself intensively to information architecture, attribute engineering and software development projects, using different methodologies to ensure the efficiency and quality of the products I am proud to create.

I understand the importance of proposing methodologies that allow optimizing resources and improving the quality of database projects. In this sense, I highlight the data modeling and Data Warehouse standards, as well as the methodology for validating and managing data models, which are fundamental to achieve solid and reliable results.

In addition to acting as a business consultant, where I offer innovative solutions to complex problems and help organizations overcome challenges, I am also dedicated to sharing my knowledge through lectures, training, and mentoring of careers and business development.

At the same time, I am a content producer on YouTube, which allows me to disseminate ideas and dialogue with an audience eager for knowledge and innovation.

Throughout my career, I have had the privilege of publishing 32 books to date, all of which are available on Amazon's platform, providing access to a wide audience in search of in-depth knowledge and insights.

However, even though I am involved in all these professional activities, I never let go of my constant learning process, finding happiness in the little things and pursuing my true purposes of helping those who seek me.

I have a deep respect for everyone and dedicate myself to activities that transcend work, such as the study of the universe of music on the piano.

In addition, my personal life is also important to me. I have been married to my beloved wife, Andrea, since 1998, and our union is filled with happiness and companionship.

22.2 Some books published by Prof. Marcão.

Figure 54 – Some books by Prof. Marcão.

Figure 55 – Some more books by Prof. Marcão.

22.3 Books on Open Data by Prof. Marcão.

Figure 56 – Books on Open Data.

22.4 How to contact Prof. Marcão.

For lectures, training and business mentoring, please contact me on my LinkedIn profile or by email marcao.tecno@gmail.com.

It will be a pleasure to interact with you.

Prof. Marcão – MARCUS VINÍCIUS PINTO

CONSULTING | MENTORING | TRAINING | LECTURES

marcao.tecno@gmail.com

https://bit.ly/linkedin_profmarcao

Be my follower and get access to unmissable content!

Instagram: https://bit.ly/3tpZ5kp

YouTube: https://bit.ly/4ah44nT

Linkedin: https://bit.ly/linkedin_profmarcao

My Amazon Author Page: https://amzn.to/3S2xCgL

Spotify: https://spoti.fi/3c0fClN

Linktree: https://linktr.ee/tudo_prof.marcao

MY CONSULTING FIRM: https://mvpconsult.com.br/

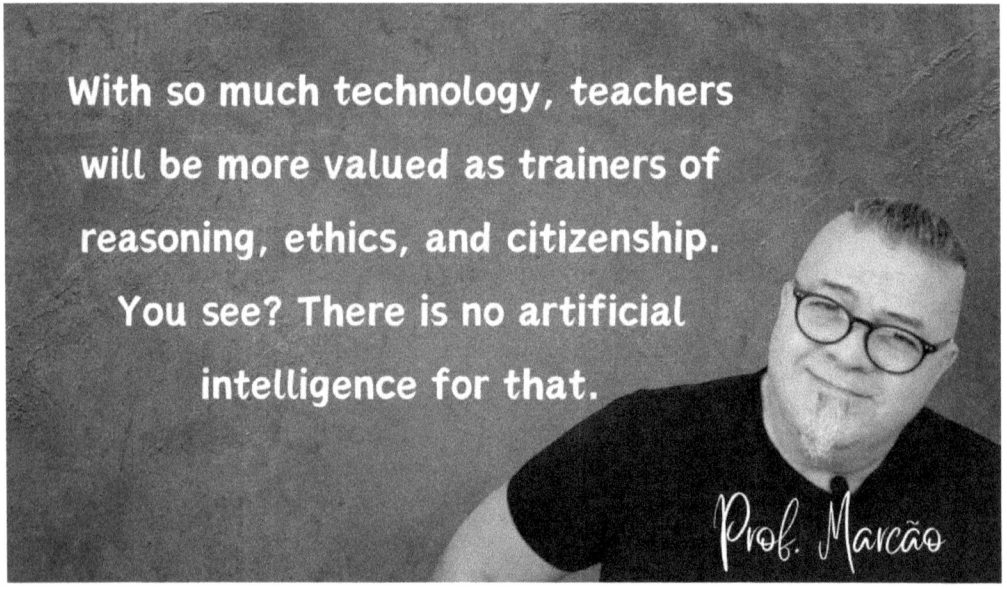

Figure 57 – Let's value teachers.

www.ingramcontent.com/pod-product-compliance
Lightning Source LLC
Chambersburg PA
CBHW062104220526
45471CB00010B/3591